Copyright 2018 by Richard A. Billows All rights reserved.

Microsoft is a registered trademark and Project and Windows are trademarks of Microsoft Corporation.

Screen shots reprinted with permission from Microsoft Corporation.

All other product names and services identified throughout this book are trademarks or registered trademarks of their respective companies. They are used throughout this book in editorial fashion only and for the benefit of such companies. No such uses, or the use of any trade name, is intended to convey endorsement or other affiliation with the book.

All rights reserved. The text of this publication, or any parts thereof, may not be reproduced in any manner whatsoever without written permission from the publisher.

ISBN: 9781731509345

Printed in the United States of America

10 9 8 7 6 5 4 3 2 1

©Copyright 2013 The Hampton Group, Inc. All Rights Reserved. May not be reproduced in any form without written permission

Healthcare Project Essentials

Table of Contents

Overview of the 5 Step 4PM Methodology 3

5-Step 4PM Process 3

Step One: Broadbrush Plan 6

   Technique #1 Defining the Project Scope .. 7

   Technique #2 Requirements & High-level Deliverable Network........................... 11

   Technique #3 Charter: Problem Avoidance.. 13

Step Two: Work Breakdown Structure... 15

   Technique #4 Using Project Software........ 18

   Technique #5 Decomposition of the Work Breakdown Structure 21

Step Three: Dynamic Schedules 25

   Technique # 6 Task Sequence 25

Step Four: Assigning People to Tasks.... 32

   Technique #7: Clear Assignments & Estimates... 32

   Technique #8 Critical Path 38

   Technique #9 Team Leadership 41

Step Five: Tracking Results 45

   Technique #10 Tracking Actuals vs. Baseline 45

   Technique #11 Problem Solving and Reporting 48

   Technique #12 Closing the Project, Making the Next Project Easier 49

About the Author................................. 51

Healthcare Project Essentials

Overview of the 5 Step 4PM Methodology

I've titled this book Healthcare Project Essentials and it's just that. We're going to take you through a five-step process for planning projects, developing a work breakdown structure, building a dynamic schedule, assigning people to tasks and tracking results.

There are things this book will not teach you. We won't deal with the statistics of risk or the alternative ways to develop work estimates or the cost accounting required for project budgets. You'll learn the essence of healthcare project management but not all of the detailed information in the Project Management Body of Knowledge (PMBOK®). I wrote this book for people running smaller projects with most of the project team coming from their own organization.

You'll also learn to use project management software in a very straightforward way. This book has many illustrations of applying our 5-step methodology in Microsoft Project®. Using project management software with this simple methodology is a big time saver so we recommend that approach. Our objective is not to spend a lot of time in the software. I designed the methodology so you spend only an hour or two developing the plan & schedule and then 10 or 15 minutes a week using the software to update it. You'll spend the rest of your time managing the project.

In sum, Healthcare Project Essentials teaches you basic-level project management tools and techniques. It's appropriate for smaller healthcare projects and teams with a few people from different functional departments. Our more advanced publications like Managing Healthcare Projects, Managing Information Technology Projects, Managing Construction Projects and Advanced Project Management Techniques address the techniques required for managing larger, more complex projects.

5-Step 4PM Process

We've listed the 5 steps in the process on the chart on the next page along with the 12 best practices techniques you will learn. We're going to take you through a five-step process for planning projects, developing a work breakdown structure, building a dynamic schedule, assigning people to tasks and tracking results.

As you move through those five steps, you'll learn 12 best practice techniques for delivering projects on time. You'll go through the process of working with the hospital administrators and other interested parties who will be affected by your project (we'll call them project stakeholders).

The 12 best practice techniques you'll learn are:

1. Defining the Project Scope As a Measured Business Result
2. Decomposing the Scope into a Deliverable Network

Healthcare Project Essentials

3. Avoiding Problems with the Project Charter
4. Using Project Software in 10 Minutes a Week
5. Decomposing Deliverables into a Work Breakdown Structure
6. Sequencing Your Tasks to Finish As Early As Possible
7. Making Clear Assignments to Your Project Team
8. Using the Critical Path to Optimize Your Schedule
9. Leading a High-Performance Team
10. Using the Baseline to Spot Problems Early
11. Solving Problems and Reporting to Hospital Administrators
12. Closing Projects to Make the Next One Easier

Copyright 2013. The Hampton Group, Inc. All rights reserved. May not be reproduced in any form without written permission.

Healthcare Project Essentials

Key Outputs from the 5-step Process

Broadbrush Project Plan

The Broadbrush Plan is a concise 1½-page document for project initiation. It allows executives to make decisions and exercise strategic control over projects and the business value they produce. It also provides them with hard-edged metrics for measuring performance and the quality of the deliverables.

Scope & High-Level Deliverable Network

This network of deliverables is the path from where you are now to where you want to be, which is the scope of the project. Every entry in the network is a deliverable that you define with a metric. The metric tells everyone what you will produce and how you will define success.

Work Breakdown Structure Decomposition

Rather than creating mindless "to do" lists, project managers (PMs) craft work breakdown structures by breaking down the scope into a high-level deliverable network of measurable results that become peoples' accountabilities. Every team member's assignment is in the form of a measurable business outcome so their accountability is crystal clear. The resulting WBS is compact so the PM can control the scope and update it quickly and control the project scope. You will support each entry with a work package that makes the details clear so they miss nothing. The PM and the hospital administrators have unambiguous checkpoints to measure progress.

Dynamic Project Scheduling

PMs use dynamic project scheduling techniques that let them update plans in just minutes each week and quickly model alternatives to cut duration, lower budgets and adjust the business value a project produces. These techniques give hospital administrators the hard data they need for decision-making and consideration of alternatives.

Status Reporting with Clear Checkpoints

With weekly tracking, PMs and hospital administrators have hard-edged checkpoints to measure progress. They can anticipate problems and implement corrective action early, when it costs the least. PMs make concise status reports on projects and always offer alternatives for the administrators to consider.

Healthcare Project Essentials

Step One: Broadbrush Plan

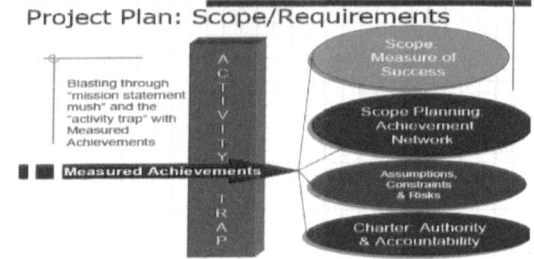

You will start your project management work by defining the scope of the project with the hospital administrator. That is, you'll define the business objective the hospital administrator wants the project to deliver. When you set about defining the scope during project planning there are a number of traps to avoid. One trap is thinking about what you have to do rather than the project's end results. Thinking about the activities you need to complete is much easier than thinking about the business outcome the project should produce. This is the activity trap where you focus on the details and ignore the project's business purpose. In the activity trap, a PM receives a project assignment, thinks about the first thing to do and starts work, figuring to think about the next step when they come to it.

Sometimes, PMs cloak their descent into the activity trap by writing a long and flowery mission statement for the project. This does no harm unless it is a substitute for politely pushing the hospital administrator to make the hard "end result" decisions up front. You need to specify exactly what the project **will** deliver and what it **will not** deliver. The hospital administrator has to make this decision and tell you how he will judge the success of the project. Being that explicit at the beginning may cause some discussion and disagreement but it is far better to work through those conflicts before you start work rather than discovering the success measures when you are almost done. Unfortunately, the activity trap snares so many PMs that it is one of the two leading causes of project failure. The activity trap wastes resources and frustrates project team members with continuously changing assignments. The lure of the activity trap, that bottomless pit, has ruined countless projects.

Top-Down Project Planning

You'll avoid the activity trap with a 1-2 page document, called the Broadbrush plan, which covers the big-picture decisions that are required before you can start your project. When the hospital administrator approves the Broadbrush plan, the Initiation phase of the project is complete. The key to this process is to avoid those delicious technical details that quickly drag you into the "activity trap." Your focus during a Broadbrush planning process is to provide the hospital administrator with the opportunity to make decisions about the end

Healthcare Project Essentials

results the project will produce. Your focus is on the measured business-relevant outcomes not the details of how you will achieve them. You also want to secure the hospital administrator's decisions on the authority you'll need to manage the project team. You keep the document short and high-level so you engage their attention. You can develop long formal plans later when the hospital administrator has approved the strategy.

A Broadbrush project plan is never long but requires thought, decisions and agreement on three things:

1. Project Scope - an unambiguous measurement of the project's outcome. For example, "Answer 90% of our customers' inquiries in 120 seconds or less with no more than 5% callbacks on the same problem."

2. High-level Deliverable Network (HLD) - a hierarchical network of measured deliverables that leads to the scope.

3. Project Charter – a short narrative covering risks, assumptions, constraints, resource requirements, change control, and PM authority.

Collectively, these elements define our project scope, requirements and charter. Your organization may also require other narrative documents but the elements above are critical for controlling projects and achieving success. They are the strategic foundation for a successful project.

Technique #1 Defining the Project Scope

Scope: Measure of Success

An objectively verifiable business outcome
- Clarity on what the sponsor wants
- Scope change control
  - Clarifies what is included in the project
  - What is excluded because it's not necessary
- Clear team performance expectations

PMs need to drive projects from quantifiable scope definitions. Driving a project plan from the success measures keeps the focus where it should be; on achieving the end result. By working with the hospital administrator to define success before the project starts, the PM is in a much better position to control the project.

As an example, let's say the Human Resources Director for a medium-sized hospital, contacts you about doing a project. She says, "I know that this is not your specialty but you are the only project manager I know. I need your help. Our personnel records, paper and electronic, are so out-of-date that it takes us days to find out what department a person works in. On top of that, employees' quarterly performance reviews are useless, if they get them at all. I want you to straighten out that whole mess so when a line manager calls, we can find up-to-date employee

Healthcare Project Essentials

personnel records on the system and quickly give them the data they want. We may also need some remodeling of our office to make all this work. And we want the employee reviews to give solid, detailed feedback on their performance."

You finished writing some notes, wishing you could stick with your kind of project. Then the Human Resources Director went on, "You can use anyone you want to get this done. This is a high priority. You'll probably have to involve five or six people from our group, some department managers and someone from IT, Administration and Facilities so you get a lot of good input. Decide on how to organize the files and what standards the performance reviews should meet. A good place to start is probably by updating all the records. Then maybe you can draft a memo, for my signature, telling managers that they have to do performance reviews on time and give their people useful feedback on their performance and developmental needs. You get the team put together and we will figure out the rest of the project from there."

The Human Resources Director has given you a lot of information about this project and what you're supposed to do. It would be very easy to start work on the files and draft that memo. However, all of the information is in the form of activities. The Human Resources Director hasn't told you what end result she wants. To succeed with this project, you have to know how the Human Resources Director is going to measure the success of the project when you're done. That definition will give you a tool to control the scope of the project and decide what should, and what should not, be included in the project work.

So, you have to ask the Human Resources Director some questions to get at the business purpose of the "laundry list" of changes that she talked about. You might start by asking, "After the files are up to date and managers are doing thorough performance reviews on time for all the employees, what will that do for us?"

She answers, "We'll be on top of things!"

You sense the Human Resources Director is getting just a little bit angry at the questions but you press on because if you don't find out what problem the Human Resources Director wants to solve and how she will measure success, you have almost no chance of delivering it. So you continue.

"If I know exactly what end result you want, I can do a good job and give you exactly what you want. So let me ask this, three months after we finish this project, what will be different; what will you expect to see?"

"Okay," the Human Resources Director sighs and then pauses for a moment to think. "Three months after the project's done, I won't have managers complaining to me that we don't know what's going on and how it takes forever to get employee information from us."

Now the Human Resources Director is talking about end results instead of activities so you know you're on the right track. But you have to change these end results into metrics.

You ask, "So if I understand what you want, the employee records have to be current. How current? Would five days be good enough?"

The Human Resources Director thinks for a moment and says, "No, we can do better than that. Let's say the personnel system is never more than 3 days behind."

Healthcare Project Essentials

> You make a note and then ask, "With the records current to within 3 days, how fast do we have to answer a line manager's questions about our people?"
>
> "That's a hard one," the Human Resources Director says, frowning in thought. "Some complex data requests will take time- a day or two, others just a few seconds."
>
> "Well, how about we set the goal at 80% of the requests are answered in 10 minutes or less?"
>
> The Human Resources Director grins and says, "How about 95%?"
>
> You smile back and say, "It will take a lot longer to get that close to perfection. What percentage are we answering within 10 minutes now?"
>
> The Human Resources Director frowns again and says, "About 1%. Let's go with 80%; that'll be a great improvement."

What you've done in this planning session is to get agreement on the scope of the project. You now have an unambiguous scope defined with a metric. You have quantified the Human Resources Director's expectations for the project and you will use it to drive the planning process. . You've also given yourself a tool for controlling changes to the scope of the project. When the Human Resources Director was talking about objectives like "straightening up the records" and "being on top of things" it's very hard to decide what is, and what is not, a change in the scope. With a measurable deliverable to quantify your scope, controlling scope creep is much easier.

Activity Trap: Project Death Spiral

- We focusing only on what to do next... not the outcomes we want at the end
- ◆ Activities are so easy to list, that we think are making progress
- ◆ A sound project plan is not a list of attractive features or good ideas

In this example, you avoided the activity trap in the discussion with the Human Resources Director, but it is such an obstacle to project success that we should delve into it in a bit more detail. The deadly lure of the activity trap defeats many efforts to clarify the scope of projects during initial planning. This initial planning phase is the point at which a Project Manager (PM) and the hospital administrator can easily fall into the activity trap. The hospital administrator usually has a few ideas about features and the first several steps for you to do and then says, "It's time to get going on that project and start work immediately." That "start fast and plan later" approach is a project killer.

Why? Everyone has a list of good ideas and activities that you can make into a long "To Do" list. You can hope that these activities improve performance and hope the result satisfies the hospital administrator. But there's entirely too much hoping going on here. In the activity trap, the project manager has no way to measure when the tasks are successfully completed. How does the PM decide what tasks to include or how much time and resources to invest in each of them?

Healthcare Project Essentials

Politics and power alone will determine what's in the project and it will forever be a moving target.

The main problem is that none of the activities connects with a deliverable. Because the PM never asked the hospital administrator to define success, the PM is in a situation where the hospital administrator will define success as the project progresses or at its conclusion. Worse, the definition of success will be a moving target and people will change it to move the effort in directions they favor.

The project manager and the hospital administrator have fallen into the "activity trap." They'll add new activities each week rather than driving the project plan toward the scope. They buried themselves in the minutia of tasks rather than focusing on the end result. They added tasks to the plan because they sounded good or they had used them before. The project won't solve the business problem that triggered it.

Healthcare Project Essentials

Technique #2 Requirements & High-level Deliverable Network

The scope is not the last measured deliverable we'll develop, but it is the most important and the most difficult to conceive. With the hospital administrator's approval of the scope, the project manager can begin decomposing it into high-level deliverables that lead to the scope. The high-level deliverables are not activities; they are also measured business results. You don't think about how you're going to do the work, you simply identify the major measured results which will carry you from where you are now to where you need to be; the project scope.

Let's continue with our example and see how you need to handle the development of the high-level deliverables for the HR department project, using the scope the Human Resources Director has approved.

Sometimes, you'll sit down and lay out the requirements for a project yourself. Other times, you'll involve the project team in the process. Let's start by thinking it through, develop some requirements ideas and then show them to the team. To reach the project's scope, "80% of the info requests answered in 10 minutes," the Human Resources Director gave you a few ideas:

- The records have to be current on personnel actions

- Managers have to turn their quarterly performance reviews in on time

- The performance reviews have to be thorough

- HR staff has to know how to efficiently answer inquiries in the system.

With these ideas in mind, you might start talking to a number of other people, including line managers, HR staff, facilities and the IT department, to flesh out the deliverables. Each of these discussions starts with you acquainting everybody with the project scope. These discussions are another opportunity to dive headfirst into the activity trap and all those delicious ideas. You keep the conversations on track by talking about end results. If people think the requirements make sense, then you work to convert them into measured deliverables.

Let's take one of the requirements, "The performance reviews have to be thorough," as an example. Now that is an activity and you'll have to convert it into a measured deliverable. That's your normal process. You think through the activity and then convert it into a measured deliverable. You might talk to some managers and find that they don't know what should be in a "thorough" performance review or how to do it. This gives you some ideas.

You talk to the Human Resources Director and get a list of 17 items that are required for a thorough employee performance review. Another requirement is to train the managers on how to complete those reviews. From this thinking, you might come up with an end result like "95% of the quarterly reviews contain the 17 required items." That's your high-level deliverable, and to support it you'll need sub-deliverables for developing and getting approval of the standard. How do you measure that requirement? Maybe the management committee should approve the review standard. So you'll assign a team member to develop the performance review standards and that assignment will produce a measured business

Healthcare Project Essentials

outcome of "Management committee approves 17 item performance review standard."

You also need to train the managers in doing performance reviews that meet the standard. How do you measure training? You think through the purpose of the training, which is to increase the managers' competency in doing employee performance reviews. Then you think about how you will assess the training program you finish it. Last, you think about how you would measure if the training succeeded. You might decide that a test at the end of training is the best way to measure its effectiveness. That might lead to a deliverable of "90% of the managers score 80% or higher on a test of the performance review standards."

The thinking you've gone through is to gather ideas on your requirements then transform them into measured deliverables. You think about the activity and how you will assess the assignment when the team member finishes it. The criteria you will use in assessing the completed assignment becomes your measured deliverable. Conceiving measured deliverables is difficult for everybody because we are all so accustomed to activity lists. But the thinking investment leads to everyone knowing what you expect of them before they start work.

The completed high-level deliverable network, with the deliverables subdivided, is below. This is a very simple looking document, reflecting a great deal of thought. When the Human Resources Director approves this network, you can proceed with the rest of the plan.

Completed Deliverable Network

The graphic above shows the requirements for the project in deliverable network form. You'll use this deliverable network as the backbone of your project plan after the Human Resources Director has approved it.

With the scope and high-level deliverables defined, you can move on to the other components of your charter.

Healthcare Project Essentials

Technique #3 Charter: Problem Avoidance

The risk section of the Charter is the place to identify potential issues concerning resources and politics. Uncovering the assumptions underlying a deliverable requires some thought. Below are a few risks for your project. Note that you've stayed at the business results level and avoided those pointless assumptions like, "everyone will do their task on time." Instead, you have focused on what can cause the project to fail:

1. Notifications of missed review dates from HR do not cause managers to turn their reviews in on time.
2. Managers and their bosses don't do reviews that meet the approved standards.

That's it. You may add another one or two but the point here is to keep the list short so the risks to the project's success get the attention they deserve.

Assumptions, Constraints & Risks

- Risk assessment and avoidance
- Assumptions about customer or employee behavior and reactions
- Politics, conflict and messy turf issues
- Covers only the "show-stoppers" that threaten the MOS™

Copyright 2013. The Hampton Group, Inc. All rights reserved. May not be reproduced in any form without written permission.

Healthcare Project Essentials

With the scope, a high-level network of deliverables and risks, you can complete the plan by proposing to the hospital administrator the authorities you will need to manage the project.

Authority, Resources & Change Control

- People we need
- Their availability
- Our authority to manage
  - Directly assign work to project team members
  - Evaluate performance
  - Reward performance
- Scope change control

It's time to do a little thinking on the resources you need and your authority to manage them. You'll use your deliverable network for this and it shows the deliverables you'll need from many other people. When you subdivide the high-level deliverables, you involve people from other organizational units who will produce some of the deliverables.

Now not all the people who'll be on the team work for you. Many may have the same boss but you don't have any formal authority to assign them work or evaluate their performance. They all have other jobs besides working on the project.

So your project charter aims at getting the hospital administrator to help you secure the resource and the authority to manage them. You'll want to avoid going to the hospital administrator every time a team member's assignment is late. So you establish your authority now to avoid problems later.

You ask for the resources you need and the authority to manage them during the planning process because your chances of getting some level of authority are far better now than if you wait until you have a problem with a team member.

> In the charter for our example HR project, you'll ask for resources and authority. For a trainer named Jill, you might say, "I need approximately 50 hours of Jill's time during the next 60 days to develop and deliver the performance review training. Please adjust her workload to make these hours available and tell her that I will be assigning her work within that 50-hour block of time. Also, my evaluation of her work will be considered in her quarterly performance review." You may not always get that authority but it's worthwhile to ask for it.

Another part of the charter is your recommended procedure for controlling changes to the scope of the project. This process should include documentation of the requested change, analysis of the impact on scope, time, cost and resources, which the hospital administrator accepts or rejects.

Healthcare Project Essentials

Broadbrush Plan Approval

- Scope – Measure of Success
- Requirements – Achievement network
- Charter
  - Assumptions, Constraints & Risks
  - Resources
  - Authorities
  - Change Control Mechanism
- Approval lets us start scheduling

Charter Plan Approval

With the preceding elements of the plan complete, you are ready for the first of your project presentations. At this first meeting, you're looking for the hospital administrator to approve your charter & strategy for the project. Some hospital administrators want a detailed schedule and a final commitment on the completion date at this first session. But you are far better off to get approval of the high-level plan and then develop the details. There are several reasons for taking this two-step approach:

First, putting a schedule together is a lot of work. You avoid redoing it by getting the hospital administrator's approval on the scope and charter before you put the schedule together. Second, when you present a schedule people tend to dive into the details and you want some attention paid to the big picture. This session need not be a long meeting, particularly if you've been showing the hospital administrator the pieces as you finish them. But the two-step approval process is the better way to do it.

Step Two: Work Breakdown Structure

With the charter approved, you can continue the top down planning process with another level of decomposition, if necessary. The charter provides you with an approved network of deliverables, each of which ties to the project's overall scope. If the assignments are too large, you can decompose them further. This creates a work breakdown structure (WBS).

Now, you're ready to dive into the software without abandoning the idea of measured deliverables. You do not write long laundry lists of every possible thing people can think of. Instead of viewing the work breakdown structure as a "To Do" list, you need to view it as a list of the deliverables your team is accountable for producing. That's how you'll manage the project and the assignments within it. On 1-person projects, you can list all the activities and be reasonably accurate in identifying everything you need to do (i.e. planting your herb garden or a small improvement project).

But when the projects get bigger, you want to build a small project plan that is easy to keep current and which focuses on the deliverables they are accountable for producing, not every nit-picky sub-task.

Now, many hospital administrators are accustomed to seeing monstrously long and highly detailed work breakdown structures. It is not unusual to see a 3-month project with a team of 5 have 400 or more lines in the work breakdown structure. While this may look impressive at the start, and may convince

Healthcare Project Essentials

people that the PM is "really in control of what's going to happen," this is a fantasy.

What happens to these monstrously detailed work breakdown structures? They create project plans that are very time-consuming or impossible to maintain. In fact, so many of those detailed tasks change each week that it takes too much time to update the project plan, so the PM doesn't do it. This leaves them with no tool to manage the project. They may have impressed the hospital administrator at the beginning with all the details but they cannot exercise control over what's happening, spot problems or fix them.

Even worse, these monstrously detailed work breakdown structures undermine the commitment and accountability of the project team. If you assign people a To Do list, that's all they take responsibility for completing. Without much thought, they complete the list of items on their To Do list, having no sense of responsibility for the deliverable that should result at the end of their work. Only the project manager is responsible for end results. This is another example of micro-management. You want project team members to feel accountable for producing a business result and solving the problems they encounter along the way, not just completing a checklist.

You do have standard procedures to follow in many types of projects. But all the steps in a standard procedure shouldn't be in the project plan. You can craft a measured deliverable of completing the required 17 steps and leave the details in the procedure manual. Completing those 17 steps is important and part of the deliverable but why track each one?

Now, not everybody can successfully complete a large deliverable that takes 10 days, without detailed instructions. For some members of your project team, assignments of two or three days are better. For other members of the project team, small assignments will not engage their interest or commitment. As we will discuss later, you have to craft assignments that are the "right" size for each of the people on your project team. But the answer is not to give everybody a highly detailed To Do list of 1-day tasks.

You may be saying to yourself, "But they won't know what to do." Again, if you want people to follow a standard operating procedure in completing their assignments, as is often the case, then you should make adhering to the procedure part of the deliverable. But this does not mean that you must write the entire procedure into the work breakdown structure. As an example, if your organization has test procedures, you can assign an engineer to that deliverable stated as "meet all of the test requirements on page 26 of the procedure manual." You don't need to list all of those required steps.

In sum, you want to design the work breakdown structure as a listing of the deliverables you will hold people accountable for producing. This will give you a small project schedule which people will be able to look at and understand. As importantly, you will be able to update it in 10 or 15 minutes per week and always have the up-to-date version of the project schedule from which you can answer people's questions. This approach is far better than developing a monstrous project plan, which may impress people at the beginning but which proves useless in managing your project, reporting status or in developing solutions to the project's problems.

Now, let's discuss the project management software.

Healthcare Project Essentials

Technique #4 Using Project Software

How We Use the Software

- ◆ Not a spreadsheet or word processor
- ◆ It's a dynamic computer model of:
  - Task durations
  - Dependencies between tasks
  - The project's duration
- ◆ Every time we make a change it automatically optimizes the schedule to finish as early as possible

An effective method of learning is to enter the following project plans into the Microsoft Project® software.

We'll tackle the use of project software in the following sequence:

1. Develop the Work Breakdown Structure (WBS)
2. Create a predecessor network
3. Assign people and estimate work
4. Obtain schedule approval
5. Track actual results and solve problems.

Throughout this process, you'll use the software as a tool to manage the project, not to list all the micro-tasks in it. Accordingly, you'll create a work breakdown structure (WBS) of people's deliverables. Then you'll combine these with predecessor relationships between deliverables. Finally, you'll assign people to the deliverables with an estimate of the amount of work and let the software calculate the duration. That calculated duration reflects the required hours of work and the availability of your people to complete it. So you'll start with a project plan that based on work estimates and resource availability, not start and finish dates picked out of the air.

You may be used to entering start and finish dates. However, resource-driven scheduling as outlined above is a far superior technique. Whenever you have a change to the work or a person's availability, the software will update the whole schedule dynamically. We will talk later about making work estimates and managing team members' utilization.

Start Date

When you open Microsoft Project® or click {File} {New}, you see a blank project document. To set the start date of the project, go to {Project} then {Project Information}. The only date you'll enter is the start date of the project. The software will calculate the finish date for you after you do your plan. You usually want to finish a project as soon as possible so leave the setting "Schedule from: Project Start Date" as it is on the graphic. You'll also use the standard calendar for the moment so leave that alone too. To get to this screen at any time, click on {Project} then {Project Information}. From here, you can click {Statistics} to get a summary of your project.

Healthcare Project Essentials

For now, let's enter the start date, or our best guess about the start date, and move on. You can always change the start date later and setting it up this way will allow the whole plan to adjust automatically.

Setting the Start Date

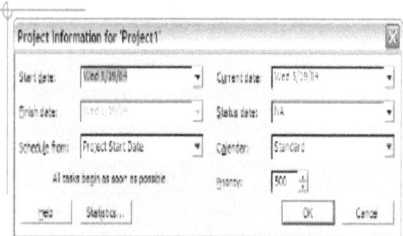

Summary & Subtasks

Summary & Subtasks

Summary tasks are "holding tanks" for
- Work
- Duration of the tasks indented under them

On the WBS, you have summary tasks with subtasks indented underneath them. The summary tasks are in bold. Summary tasks are holding tanks. You don't assign resources, enter work, durations, start/finish dates or predecessors to a summary task. When you move to tracking actuals, you'll enter completed work only for subtasks. The system rolls-up information from the subtasks and reports it for their summary task. This is easy to forget but summary tasks are the "subtotals" in our project plan. You'll use them for high-level reporting. Again, a summary task has subtasks under it. That's the definition.

In detailing your project network, there are no magic rules about how many tasks to have. A common error, as we've discussed, is to have too many. Planning with deliverables rather than activities, helps reduce the number of

Copyright 2013. The Hampton Group, Inc. All rights reserved. May not be reproduced in any form without written permission.

Healthcare Project Essentials

tasks. Think of tasks as important deliverables in the project that you wish to track.

Getting to Our Data Entry Screen
Setting the Task Entry View

There are hundreds of ways to enter and display information in Microsoft Project®. You're going to use just one view for all your data entry. You get to that view by clicking {Views} {Gantt chart} {More Views} and going down the menu, as in the graphic, until you find {Task Entry}. Highlight it and then click {Edit}. Next, put a checkmark in the little box next to "Show in menu" and the task entry view will be on the drop down list under {View}.

Healthcare Project Essentials

The Task Entry Screen
The Task Entry screen is a split screen view. The upper part shows you the Gantt chart of the project. When you highlight a task on the WBS (row #7), you see the details of that task in the lower half of the window.

In the lower half, the left side shows whom you assigned to the task and the right side show the predecessors of that task. While this takes a bit of getting used to, the task entry view lets you do everything you need to set up a project schedule. You will also use it for tracking.

Task Entry Screen

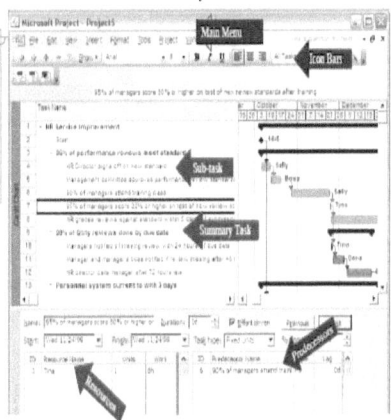

Technique #5 Decomposition of the Work Breakdown Structure

With the task entry view in place, you enter your high-level deliverables and their sub-deliverables in the "task name" column in the

Work Breakdown Structure

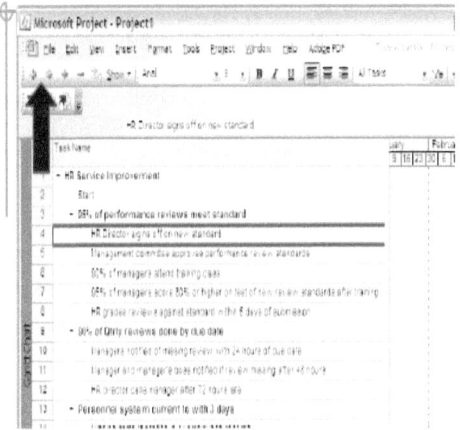

upper half of the screen. To give yourself easily accessible totals, the first line of the WBS should be the name of the project. You'll make this a summary task by indenting every other row in the project under it. Then all your reports will have the project totals on the first line.

On the second row of the WBS, enter a task called "Start." Later you'll give this task a zero duration making it a milestone. Every task that starts on the first day of the project will have "Start" as a predecessor.

Use the right pointing arrow on the second row of the icon bar (see the arrow pointing to it), to indent "Start." Indenting "Start" also makes the task above it a summary task. On the third line, you'll enter your first high-level deliverable (HLD) and use the right pointing arrow to indent it once, so it has the same indentation as "Start."

Next, you'll enter your sub-deliverables under the first high-level deliverable and indent them one tab more. When you enter the second sub-deliverable, the software will continue the previous indentation. You'll continue and enter the rest of the sub-deliverables until you come to the second high-level deliverable. Now you have to "out dent" this HLD once, so that it matches the indentation of the first HLD and you do that with the left pointing arrow. You continue with the rest of the HLD's and sub-deliverables until you have entered the whole plan. The scope for the project is the last line of the plan. You indent it the same amount as a high-level deliverable but in small projects, it usually has no sub-deliverables under it. That's all there is to the data entry of the WBS.

Healthcare Project Essentials

WBS & Our Deliverables

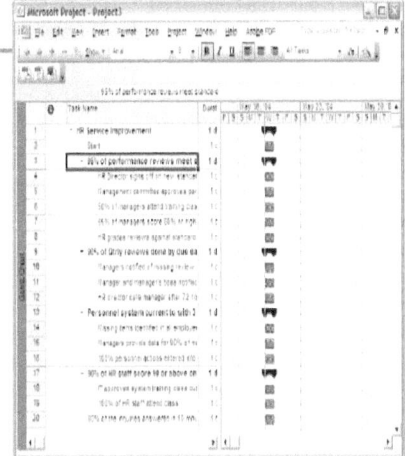

Here is the completed WBS for the Human Resources project example. Notice how all the task bars line up in a column. By default in the software, they all have a duration of one day and start on the start date of the project. You'll change this later as you build the plan.

Now this is a small project plan with 20 rows. It's easy to see what has to happen and it will be easy to update. Could you make it bigger? Sure, but you'll add more detail only when you need to add it to make assignments more clear.

Healthcare Project Essentials

Assignments & Micro-management

This work breakdown structure may be very different from what you see at work. It sets up the project manager to hold the people on the project team accountable for end results, not all the steps in getting there. Is this project manager taking terrible risks? Not really. Project managers who hold project team members accountable for their end results are PMs who get the most from the people on the project team. They trust people to a reasonable degree. Within the scope of the deliverable they have crafted for the individual, the PM trusts the person to deliver it. And remember, it is the PM who controls the "size" of the assignment and thus the degree to which each team member will be trusted.

A micro-managing PM is just the opposite. This type of PM trusts no one and feels that he has to watch everybody closely because they will do the wrong thing if not monitored. Think back to micro-managing bosses you may have had. How much enthusiasm did you bring to the job? How much accountability did you feel for the end results? The answer to both questions is probably very little.

Micro-managing as a PM style also limits the number of people and the size of projects that a PM can manage successfully. The micro-management technique collapses when the team gets bigger than 4-5 and/or when the micro-manager does not have more expertise than every team member does. Micro-manage works when you know more about the work than the person doing it does. If you don't, then the recipient of the micro-management gets pretty resentful of that style.

Again, think back to a time when you had a new boss who knew less about your job than you did. What was your reaction when this person tried to micro-manage you?

For all these reasons, consistently successful project managers are not micro-managers. Within the limits of each person's capability, successful project managers specify end results and leave it to the individual to figure out how to get there. They get interesting benefits with this management approach. Team members find work on the project more rewarding and they feel encouraged to use their creativity. This difference in the level of enthusiasm and commitment can be worth a great deal. You will avoid the pitfalls of micro-management when you design your work breakdown structure.

Healthcare Project Essentials

Step Three: Dynamic Schedules

Your next step is to take the WBS and add the predecessor relationships. It's important to remember that you specify only the immediate predecessors of a task. If task C cannot start until task B finishes and task B can't start until task A finishes, then C's predecessor is B and B's predecessor is A. All you need to enter is that B is C's immediate predecessor and A is B's immediate predecessor. There are a number of types of predecessor relationships:

· Finish to start - A must be finished before B can start

· Finish to finish - A and B must finish at the same time

· Start to start - A and B must start at the same time

· Leads and Lags - any of the preceding predecessor relationships can have a time delay (lag) or time acceleration (lead).

Finish to start, lag 3 days, means task B can start 3 days after task A finishes. Let's look at each of these types and see how to enter them in the software.

Predecessor Relationships

Control the sequence and dependencies in our project network

Technique # 6 Task Sequence

Task Sequencing

◆ Tell the software what the sequence of tasks has to be
◆ Task B can't start until A is finished
◆ Using predecessors is far faster than entering start and finish dates because the software automatically updates the plan for us and optimizes the schedule

You may be used to entering start and finish dates for each task in a project plan. All that does is make more work for you. You want the software to automatically adjust dates as things change. That's how you can limit your computer time to 10 minutes a week and keep everyone informed about what's going on.

So you will build your project schedule with predecessor relationships between the tasks. Then the software can calculate the start and finish dates for each task based on its predecessors, work, and resource availability. When you make a change to the schedule, the software will recalculate every start and finish date and instantly give you a revised schedule.

Copyright 2013. The Hampton Group, Inc. All rights reserved. May not be reproduced in any form without written permission.

Healthcare Project Essentials

Entering Predecessors
To do your predecessor data entry you'll skip down to task 4 in the upper half of the window. Why skip? Because tasks 1 and 3 are summary tasks, you don't connect them to your network. Task 2 is Start; the first task in the project and it doesn't get a predecessor.

Predecessor Data Entry

filled in the name of task #2 and put FS (that means finish to start) in the Type column. In the upper half of the screen, the software has drawn a predecessor line between task 2 and 4 and it has pushed task 4 out, so it starts after 2 is finished. That's a finish to start predecessor.

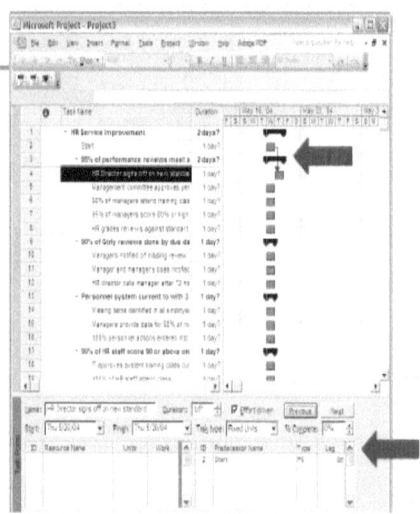

Task 4, "HR Director signs off on new standard" is a yes/no deliverable where you will develop a performance review standard and gain the Director's approval. Work on this deliverable can start on the first day of the project so you will make its predecessor Task 2, Start, by entering a "2" in the ID column. Then click OK.

Our First Predecessor
You'll see that the software has done two things. In the lower half of the screen, it has

Finish-to-Start
As you look at the screen shot from Microsoft Project®, you see the work breakdown structure and Gantt chart with bars showing the start and finish dates for each task. The data entry screen in the lower half has a list of the predecessor relationships on the right. This is the task entry screen in Microsoft Project® and you will use it for all of your data entry. Remember that you get to this view by clicking on {View}, {Gantt chart},

Copyright 2013. The Hampton Group, Inc. All rights reserved. May not be reproduced in any form without written permission.
26

Healthcare Project Essentials

{More Views} and then select {Task **Entry Screen**

The screen shot has task 5 selected in the upper half of the window. When you select it, the software frames it in black. When you click on row 5 in the upper half of the window, you see the details of that task in the lower half. Looking at the Gantt chart, you see that task 5 starts right after task 4 finishes. In fact, you can see an arrow between the end of task 4 and the start of task 5. Looking at the lower right hand quadrant of the screen, you made that happen when you entered the predecessor as task 4 as a finish-to-start (FS) type. The way you create a finish-to-start predecessor is to click the task in the upper half of the window, then enter the number of its predecessor in the lower right hand quadrant. The software will fill in the name.

Healthcare Project Essentials

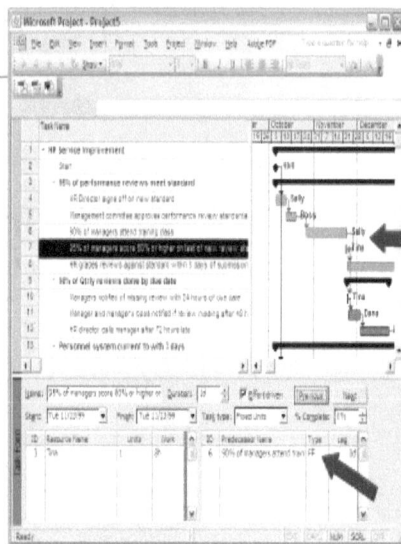

...u mean it, because the software will ...edule them that way unless the finish-to-...ish relationship will result in an over ...ocation of recourses.

... example of when you might use a finish-...finish predecessor relationship is the ...tallation of a new system in various ...iliated hospitals. This doesn't mean they'll ...start at the same date because they may ...uire different amounts of work and thus ...e different durations. But if you establish ...ish-to-finish predecessor relationships ...ween the tasks, the software will schedule ...m to finish on the same day.

Finish-to-Finish

The next kind of predecessor relationship is finish-to-finish. When you click on task 7 in the upper half of the window, you see its details in the lower half of the screen. Task 6 is the predecessor of task 7 with a predecessor type of FF, finish-to-finish. You are telling the software that you want these two tasks to finish at the same time. In fact, you're telling the software that they **must** finish at the same time. When you create a finish-to-finish predecessor relationship between two tasks, like 6 and 7, the consequences can be serious. If something happens to postpone task 6, the software will also postpone task 7 so they will still finish at the same time. When you use finish to finish relationships you must be sure

Healthcare Project Essentials

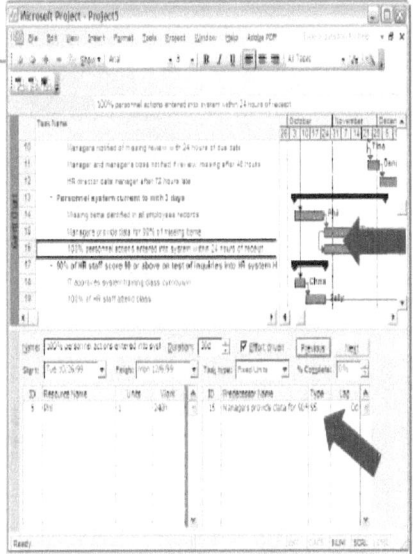

this case, if something happened to postpone the start of the newspaper ads you would want to postpone the radio and TV advertisements along with it.

Start-to-Start

The last kind of predecessor is a start-to-start relationship. Here, you're telling the software that you want the tasks to start at the same time. The same warning as we discussed with finish-to-finish holds true. When you tell the software that you want the two tasks to start at the same time and something happens to postpone the start of one, the software will postpone the other so they start at the same time.

An example of a start-to-start predecessor relationship might occur in a project where you have newspaper, TV and radio all advertising a new medical procedure. For marketing reasons, you might wish to have all three advertising campaigns running at the same time so they reinforce one another. In

Healthcare Project Essentials

Danglers in the Network

As you work your way down the work breakdown structure entering the predecessors, there is one rule you have to keep in mind. You need to close your predecessor network. Only one task in the project plan should have no successor and that is the scope. The scope is the end of the project so nothing comes after it. Every other task should have a successor. When your predecessor networks have more than one end, it can cause errors in the calculation of the duration of the entire project.

These are serious problems and so after you have built your predecessor network, and periodically thereafter, you will check the predecessor network to make sure you closed it and that the scope is the only deliverable with no successor.

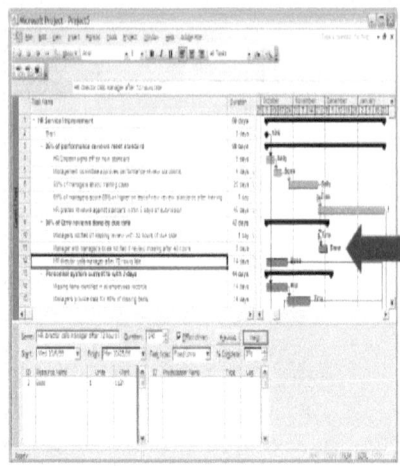

As you look at the Gantt chart, you see that task 11 has no arrow coming out of the back end. That is, task 11 has no successor. In other words, task 11 is not the predecessor of any other task in the project. Task 11 is not the project scope so it's a dangler and you need to assign a successor (e.g. make it the predecessor of some other task). The Gantt chart is not the easiest place to spot danglers. Let's look at the network diagram where it is a bit easier to spot them. You get to this chart by clicking {View} and then {Network Diagram}.

Network Diagram

To repeat, you need to have a closed predecessor network if you want the software to properly calculate the completion date of your project.

Healthcare Project Essentials

In this diagram, the lines represent predecessor relationships and the boxes are your deliverables. There is a task in the diagram that has no line coming out the back. It has no successor but it should. So it's a dangler and you need to give it a successor task. As a side note, the tasks with the shadows to the right and bottom are summary tasks and you should not connect them to the predecessor network.

When you add the missing successor, you will have a closed network and only one end-point, the project scope.

Healthcare Project Essentials

Step Four: Assigning People to Tasks

Technique #7: Clear Assignments & Estimates

Now let's assign people (resources) to tasks and estimate the amount of work required by their deliverable. There are many ways to enter resources. You'll use an easy one and you get to it by clicking on {Views}, then {More Views} and select {Task Entry} from the drop down list. Here's what you'll see. The upper half of the screen is your Gantt chart and the lower half shows the resources and predecessors of whatever task you clicked on in the upper half of the window.

You click on a task in the upper half of the window and see the details of the resources assigned to a task (lower left) and the predecessor relationships (lower right). In our example HR project, you've assigned Sally the task of developing the performance review standards and securing the Human Resources Director's approval. Now, the key step in this process is to secure Sally's commitment to the deliverable and the work estimate. You'll hurt yourself and your project if you "ram" a work estimate" down Sally's throat and create a situation where she knows she will fail before she even starts work.

You'll discuss the assignment with Sally, after you secured her involvement and availability in your project charter. The assignment sounds like it should take about two weeks because she has to talk to a variety of people to draft a new standard for performance reviews. Next you'll review it with the Human Resources Director, make any changes she suggests and get her approval. You could break this assignment into four or five smaller pieces but if Sally has done this kind of thing before, you'll give her the single, bigger deliverable. She tells you she thinks it will take 40 hours of work.

Healthcare Project Essentials

At this point, you need to set up your budgets and build estimates with your time. Let's first set up the resources. You right click on {Resources} then {team planner} and select resource sheet from the drop down list. You can set up all the resources at one time, entering their name, their max units (1.0 is full time, 0.5 if half time) and their standard and overtime pay rates (if applicable). This makes assigning them to tasks easier.

pessimistic estimate (only a 20% chance of the task taking more work) and a best guess estimate (a 50% chance of being too low). Then you enter those three numbers into the 3-point estimating tab for each task and the software calculates your work estimate at a variety of probabilities from 50% to 80% certainty. That lets you give the Human Resources Director a choice of certainty, recognizing that high certainty requires more work and thus more cost. Remember, nothing is free in project management.

You also need to work with your team members to develop work estimates. Let them give you estimates that reflect the bad risks of the assignment, which would make it take more work and the good risks which would make it take less work.

You ask each team member to give you 3 estimates: an optimistic estimate (only a 20% chance of the task taking less work), a

First Assignment

When you have Sally's agreement on the deliverable & the amount of work required, you enter the work number in the work

Healthcare Project Essentials

column in the lower half of the screen on the left hand side. You enter the work as 40 and the software assumes hours. Then you type Sally's name in the Resource Name column and then click OK.

After you clicked OK, the software did several things. First, it filled in some additional data in the lower left hand quadrant of the screen. Second, it changed the Gantt chart and increased the length of the bar for task 4. It also pushed out the start date for task 5, which is a successor of task 4. What the software did was recognize the predecessor relationship you had established between the finish of task 4 and the start of task 5. Because you told the software that task 5 could not start until task 4 had finished, the software used the duration it calculated to adjust the finish date of task 4. Then it adjusted the remainder of the project plan to reflect this information. Using this automatic updating of the project plan is much easier than having to adjust every start and finish date every time the duration estimates change. Last, the software put Sally's name on the Gantt chart so you know at a glance who's doing the work.

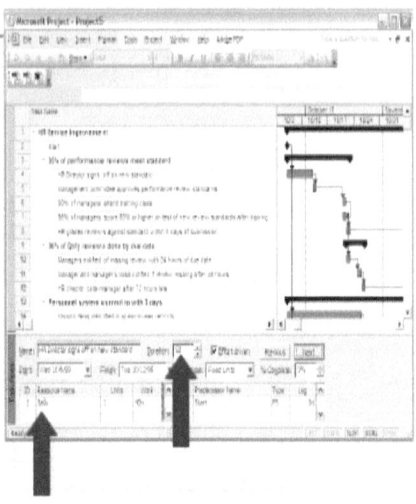

One standard in project management is that you discuss the duration of a task in terms of the number of working days that the task will take. You do not count weekends and holidays. You'll notice that Sally's task has a duration of five days but it starts on October 7 and finishes on October 13. That's seven days. However, looking at the Gantt chart you see that a weekend falls in the middle of Sally's assignment and that's why the calendar time is two days longer than the duration. This actually turns out to be very convenient because the duration of a task does not change due to weekends or holidays.

Second Assignment

The next assignment in the work breakdown structure is "Management committee approves performance review standards." You're going to assign this task to the Human Resources Director who will present the

Healthcare Project Essentials

proposed standard to the management committee and secure their approval. You need to discuss this assignment with the hospital administrator and secure their estimate of the duration it will take to get the management committee's approval.

Let's say the Human Resources Director tells you it will take five days duration to secure that approval. So, you'll type 40 into the work field, type "Boss" into the resource name field and click OK.

Third Assignment

Now let's go to task 6. You want to assign Sally to this task and so you will click into the resource name field and then single click on the arrow that comes up to the right. It shows us a list of the resources you have used so far in the project. You want to be careful not to use two different names for the same person because the software will think you have two different individuals involved when, in fact, there is only one. To avoid making this mistake after you've entered the first couple of assignments, you'll always click on the arrow to get the drop-down list and then click on the person you want to assign. To finish, you'll select Sally, enter the work and click OK.

More on the Third Assignment

You may have noted that every time you made a change in the duration of a task in the lower half of the task entry screen, the software also made adjustments to the units and work columns in the lower left-hand side. The software calculates the number of full time equivalents it will take to do the work within the indicated duration. In the screenshot you see you have one full time person, Sally, doing 160 hours of work, which the software calculates, will take 20 days.

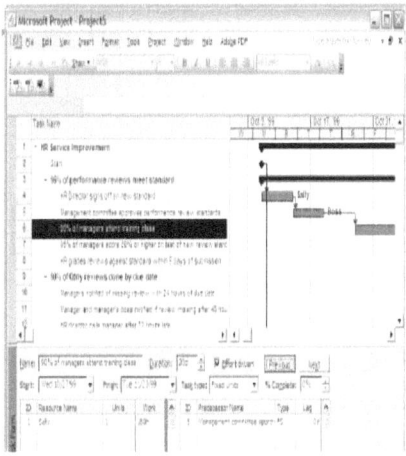

Healthcare Project Essentials

You got this result by entering 160 hours and assigning Sally to the task at the default unit, 1.0, which means she is working full-time. If she were going to work on this task halftime, you would assign her at .5 units or 50% of a full-time person.

You can assign resources to a task, enter the work and the software will calculate the duration. But when you look at the screenshot, you see that you're starting to run out of room to see the whole project as the project's overall duration increases.

Adjusting the Time Scale

You can adjust the time scale on the Gantt chart in two ways. First, you can click into the upper half of the window and then click on the "zoom out "icon (magnifying glass with a minus sign). After clicking, you'll note that the view switched from a Gantt chart that shows every day to a Gantt chart that shows every three days. By changing to a larger time scale, you can see more of the Gantt chart. If you continue to click on the zoom out icon, the Gantt chart scale will change to weeks, then months, then quarters and so on. You can also zoom in to see smaller units of time, by clicking on the zoom in icon, which looks like a magnifying glass with a plus sign in it.

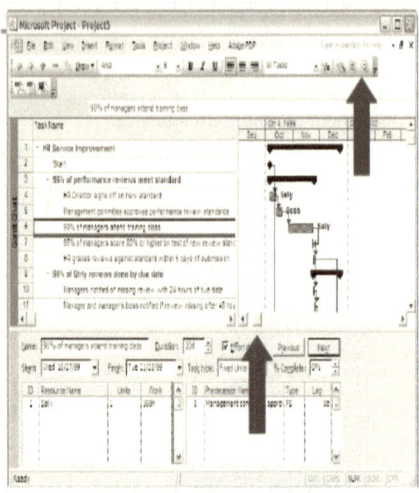

Milestones

You can proceed to assign work and resources to the rest of your tasks just as you've done for the first three assignments. There is another kind of task you want to have on the Gantt chart and that is a milestone. You make a task a milestone by entering zero in the duration field. This means that the task takes no calendar time and the software changes the symbol from a bar to a diamond, as you can see on the illustration for the task "Start". "Start" is a good example of a milestone but you don't want use too many of them since every line in our plan is a measured deliverable. A good use of milestones is to mark important dates that won't change, like the end of a warranty period or a stockholder's meeting. For these, and only these milestone tasks, you'll enter a start date. But you won't make them part of your

Healthcare Project Essentials

predecessor network. You don't enter start dates for your other tasks because that will "lock-up" the predecessor network and prevent the automatic schedule updating you want.

this is that you have parallel paths in your project plan. This is good because it means that a number of things are happening at the same time. The project will finish sooner than if only one thing was happening at a time. You'll use these parallel paths a little bit later.

Completed Gantt Chart

After you've completed the rest of your assignments and duration estimates, your project plan looks like this illustration. You're getting close to the end here and there are just a few additional adjustments you have to make before you can review the schedule with the Human Resources Director.

Before you move on, you can see that your project has several paths. All of them end with task 20, your scope. But looking at the Gantt you can see that three tasks have "Start" as a predecessor and these paths then go to tasks 4, 14 and 18. Another way of saying

Scheduling and Calendars

You've been using the standard calendar that is the default in Microsoft Project®. On that calendar, you have scheduled no work for Saturdays and Sundays. You can refine the standard workweek definition by modifying the base calendar to prohibit the software from scheduling work on holidays and other non-working days so that your project duration is realistic. To adjust the calendar for your holidays, click {Project} then {Change Working Time} and you'll see the following calendar. You can move through the

Healthcare Project Essentials

year and designate certain days as non-working time, which will cause the software to "skip" those days when scheduling the duration of a task.

It is generally worthwhile to mark your company holidays as non-working days. But it's easy to overuse customized calendars. Remember you want to build a small project plan that you can update in just a few minutes each week. Calendars are maintenance intensive and there is no sense spending 3 hours each week adjusting the calendar to reflect 1-hour department meetings and people who attend 3-hour training sessions. The issue is granularity, or the size of the hunks of deliverables you are managing in the project. If most of your team members' assignments are more than a week long, you don't need to manage the calendar at the level of 1-hour meetings. If, however, you are a real micro-manager and your assignments are at the level of 4 hours' worth of work, then prepare yourself for hours of calendar maintenance.

Technique #8 Critical Path

After you've adjusted the schedule for non-working days, you'll use the classic project management tool called the critical path. The critical path is the sequence of tasks that controls the duration of your entire project. A few pages back you looked at your Gantt chart and saw that your project had multiple paths. The longest of these paths is the critical path. It is the sequence of tasks that has the longest duration and it is critical because it controls the duration of your overall project. It makes no sense to shorten the duration of tasks that are not on the critical path because shortening those tasks will not decrease the duration of the project as a whole.

The software calculates the critical path every time you make a change in your project schedule. You can display the critical path from the menu bar by clicking on {format} and then clicking in the critical path box. The system then displays the Gantt chart with a critical path (in red on your screen).

Healthcare Project Essentials

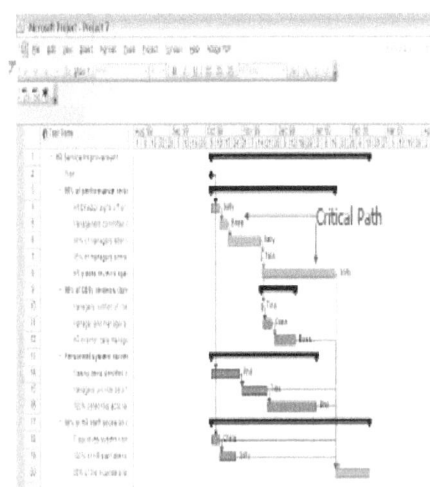

The Critical Path

The critical path is an important tool for project managers because you'll use it to shorten the duration of the project and finish earlier. Because shortening the duration is an issue on almost every project, you'll use the critical path frequently. Remember, we call it the critical path because it is the longest sequence of deliverables through the predecessor network. The critical path controls the duration of the project. The illustration shows the critical path in red. It begins on task 4, then 5, 6, 7, 8 and 20.

If the Human Resources Director wants a shorter duration, as is usually the case in all projects, you'll work to shorten the duration of only the critical path tasks. Shortening the duration of non-critical path tasks does no good in terms of shortening the project duration. So adding resources to non-critical path tasks is a waste of those resources.

If the Human Resources Director wants you to finish this project sooner, what task will you work on? The answer is task 8 because that is the longest duration task on the critical path and, thus, it is usually the best place to start. You scheduled Task 8, "HR grades reviews against the standard within 5 days" for about two months. That duration estimate was probably set to allow you enough time to give every manager feedback on the new performance reviews. How can you shorten it? You might suggest to the Human Resources Director that you change the project plan and require that every manager do a performance review on all his/her employees within 2 weeks following the training session. Then HR could check the reviews and give feedback in 4 weeks instead of 8. You may have other ideas on how to shorten this task. The one thing you don't do is just arbitrarily cut the duration. Remember you have a team member who made a commitment to finish that deliverable in 8 weeks. You will lose that commitment if you don't adjust the deliverable to realistically allow them to finish in a shorter duration.

Will cutting the duration of this task shorten the project by 4 weeks? It depends. It is possible that not all of the task reduction will ripple all the way through to the project end date. You may find that cutting the duration of task #8 takes it off the critical path. Then you might find that while you cut the duration of task #8 by 4 weeks, the project's duration is reduced by only 2 weeks.

Healthcare Project Essentials

Before you go to the Human Resources Director for final approval, you should look for opportunities to shorten the duration by altering deliverables or adding resources to tasks on the critical path. Then you'll have an answer and a trade-off when the Human Resources Director asks, "How can we finish sooner?"

Final Review & Approval
During your final review session, you will present both the approved project scope and charter as well as the detailed schedule and budget. You present both so no one forgets that the project schedule is dependent on the scope, assumptions, resources and authorities described in the charter. When you present both everybody remembers the linkages between these parts of your project plan.

You don't want to go into the final approval meeting with a mindset of "fighting for your project plan." Instead, you welcome changes but handle them as tradeoffs between scope, budget and duration. The trade-off for finishing earlier is either reducing the scope or using more resources. You'll talk about your willingness to make these trades but you're always clear that every trade has two sides. You might say, "If you take away two of my team members, the project will finish 3 weeks later. If you want to increase the scope, the project will take longer and cost more."

◆ The project is prepared with:
- Scope
- Charter
- The schedule & resource assignments

◆ Boss always says it takes too long
- Have duration trade-offs ready
- Scope control starts during the approval meeting
- Maintain the team's commitments

In summary, you are not fighting because the hospital administrators outrank you and you will not win the fight. Rather, you present the hard data upon which you have built your project plan. You agree to make any change they want as long as they understand that every change involves a trade. This approach is the way you can deliver on your project promises.

Healthcare Project Essentials

Technique #9 Team Leadership

Team leadership begins very early during planning and continues throughout the entire life of the project. We'll talk about it here not because it's a last-minute kind of thing but because the project planning and scheduling you've now completed are the foundation upon which you will lead your team. The foundation you've built solves many of the problems that project teams face. With your project scope and high-level deliverable network, you are in a good position to control the project scope. You'll avoid the typical problems project teams have with trying to hit project objectives that are moving targets. Because you've maintained your focus on measured deliverables, you're able to make assignments to your project team members so that they understand what you expect before they start work. This part of the foundation saves the project team from having to guess about what's expected. As importantly, they don't have to worry about being "blind-sided" by requirements that change at the last minute.

You have also created a situation where you can develop a reasonable degree of team member commitment to the project and their assignments. You don't gain this commitment by telling people they are committed to a due date. You gain commitment by negotiating with each team member about the deliverable you need them to produce and the hours of work it will take. In the preceding steps, you developed estimates with your team members rather than imposing them. You've also designed assignments for each person that are important deliverables in the project, not long laundry lists of micro-tasks. Thus, to the limits of their capability, you trust the members of our project team to produce deliverables within the time frame you've negotiated. The project manager who trusts people certainly takes a risk. However, taking that risk and holding people accountable for end results is an important part of the process of gaining people's commitment to the project.

You'll use your project plan and schedule to inform every member of the team about the project purpose and how their assignment contributes to achieving that end result. As you move into the tracking portion, you'll continue to give them information about how the project is doing and about changes to their assignments in the overall project schedule.

The typical situation for your project team members is that they are involved on multiple projects as well as having a "real" job. The simple steps we've outlined here go a long way toward creating a trusting environment for your project team where there is little guessing and very little uncertainty about what's expected. You can certainly add to that foundation with team building exercises and other "morale building" activities. However, when people can't find time to do their project work, demanding extra time for these kinds of activities is a burden. It's far better to give every team member clarity on your expectations and trust them to be accountable for their deliverables. That's much better than spending hours on team building activities followed by micro-management.

In addition to using your foundation properly, your leadership style with the project team has an important impact on the culture of the team. The most common types of leadership and their general pros and cons are:

Autocratic – makes unilateral decisions for everyone on the team without their input. This style takes little time but does not give the PM the benefit of the team member's expertise.

Coaching – guides team members to the correct decisions and processes. This style is time consuming but yields the benefit of enhancing the capabilities of the team members.

Consensus – builds agreement on actions using the inputs of the team members. This style is very time consuming but is powerful when the team is composed of experts in various disciplines who must all agree and who possess more expertise in their area than the PM.

Consultative – gathers inputs from the team prior to making the decision. This also requires more time than the unilateral styles but it is a powerful technique for building support from team members.

Directing – gives instructions on what to do and is an efficient style that is most appropriate for emergency situations, but it does not build team member commitment.

There is no one style that is suitable for every PM in all situations. Project managers use many of these styles in different situations and with different team members. However, trying to use a style with which you are uncomfortable is never a wise choice.

Team Culture & Conflict

Every project team develops a unique culture as the people work together. Sometimes that culture encourages interdepartmental bickering and blaming others for problems and failures. Other times the culture may encourage strict compliance with the rules and discourage creativity and innovation. Finally, other cultures encourage a strong achievement orientation with innovation and creativity to reach deliverables.

Team Culture & Conflict

- ◆ Culture of the team impacts:
   - Work attitudes (quality & productivity)
   - Commitment to assignment
- ◆ Assignments & reward style
   - Trust is reciprocated
   - Non-monetary rewards
   - Consistency in treating team performance

In every project culture, conflict will exist. You should not avoid conflict. Rather, you directly address it with problem solving behavior that you aim at the causes. You also involve the people having the conflict. You can handle conflict by using several techniques, including:

Compromise – developing a solution on which all participants can agree. While this can bring temporary solutions, the conflict may revive.

Healthcare Project Essentials

Confronting – directly addressing the problem by unearthing the causes of conflict and addressing them with the parties having the conflict. This style is the preferred style because it can lead to permanent solutions.

Forcing – This involves the use of power, authority or influence to impose a solution. This style often leads to continuing resentment and may not yield a permanent solution.

Smoothing – addressing the points of similarity rather than those of contention. This style minimizes the conflict while emphasizing the points of agreement. It is usually a short-term solution.

Withdrawal – avoiding the problem by backing away from the conflict situation. It also does not offer a permanent solution.

While every member of the team influences the culture, the project manager's style is of paramount importance. Specifically, how you make assignments and what behavior you reward have an important impact on the overall team culture. If you make assignments to people with a style that shows you don't trust them and have no confidence in their ability to perform, it should not come as a surprise that they feel no sense of accountability for their project work. When you don't hold people accountable for solving at least some of the problems they encounter, you shouldn't be surprised when they bring every problem to you for resolution.

Project managers usually don't have monetary rewards to hand out to project team members for successful completion of assignments. But this does not mean that you don't have any rewards whatsoever. You always have the option of buying lunch for a team member who completes an assignment early or achieves more than you asked. But even if you don't have the budget to buy lunch, you still have a very powerful reward in our public praise of high achievers. And you can make lunch or your praise worth something to your team members if you're careful about how you use it. If you praise everybody all the time, your praise quickly becomes valueless. Why is it valueless? Because the people know they have done nothing to earn it. If, on the other hand, you consistently praise people who finish on time and people who finish early but do not give public praise for trying hard or having a good excuse, then you make your praise valuable to your project team members. Given that you usually have no other formal reward beyond that lunch or public praise, it's important to maintain its value.

While you never want to criticize a team member publicly, it is okay not to praise everybody. Thus, if two of your team members have finished early and three are late on their assignments, you will publicly praise the two who have finished early and say nothing publicly about the other three. This approach can be difficult to implement because you're concerned about "hurting people's feelings." But if you praise people just so they won't feel badly, your praise is soon worth nothing.

In summary, the way you manage the project team in terms of assignments and rewards is a primary determinant of the culture of the project team. One of the most difficult things about project management is to maintain a

Healthcare Project Essentials

consistent style with the project team when things are going badly. Yet a good project manager insulates the team from the hospital administrator's displeasure by allowing individuals who have delivered their assignments on time to feel successful, even if there are problems with other parts of the project.

Healthcare Project Essentials

Step Five: Tracking Results

After all the work you've invested in setting up a project plan and establishing a schedule and budget, it's time to use that foundation to actually manage your project. Microsoft Project® software provides a number of analytical tools for tracking progress. The hardest part is often getting the status information from the team. Project team members are often less than diligent about submitting progress reports. But without them, a project manager is flying blind. It's never too early to make it clear how important progress reports are and how you're more than willing to adopt extreme measures (nagging, flogging, assault & battery) to receive them on time. You can also make it easier for the team members. Because of the way you've built your plan, the only data you need is the following numbers for each in-process task:

- % Completed
- Actual work completed
- Work Remaining.

Most projects are worthy of weekly progress reports from the people working on all in-process tasks. With data available on this frequency, you'll avoid nasty surprises at the end.

Tracking Results

You also position yourself to solve small problems early rather than big problems late. By having status data updated and available weekly, you're able to take corrective action early and to "keep your hands off" tasks and people that are doing well. Constantly checking progress can quickly transform your style into micro-management.

The first step is to "save the baseline" by storing the approved budget and schedule so you can compare your actuals to it. Remember that every time you enter actuals, the system will change the task start and finish dates based on what has happened to each task and its predecessors. Having a stored copy of the original plan is the basis for your tracking analysis.

Technique #10 Tracking Actuals vs. Baseline

Your first step after the Human Resources Director has approved the plan is to save the baseline and preserve your ability to compare what's actually happened to what you planned. The baseline includes every task, start date, finish date, resource assignment

Healthcare Project Essentials

and work estimate in the project. You can save several versions of the baseline, but you'll usually save just one. With this "snapshot" of the plan saved before you start work, you're set to track progress for the duration of the project. Comparing actual performance to the baseline is the best way to develop your status reports.

Saving the Baseline

After the Human Resources Director has approved the project, you'll save the baseline like this: Click on {Project} then on {Set Baseline}. A new window will pop up. Make sure you fill in the "Save Baseline" and "Entire Project" buttons, and then click OK. You have saved the baseline. There is now a "Polaroid picture" of your entire project saved on your PC. As you enter changes and actuals, this baseline version of the plan will not change so you can always compare the original plan to your current schedule.

Creating the Baseline

- The baseline is our basis of comparison between actuals and every (date, task and predecessor the sponsor approved
- Tracking is very date sensitive so we need to record actual status on the "as of" date of the status reports

Status Reports

Before you enter status data, you need to tell the system the date your team reported the status reports. Click {project} then "status date" and enter the "as of" date of the reports.

Let's jump ahead in time to the end of the first week of work on your project. You have three tasks that should have started. With a little nagging, you get all three status reports almost on time. Even though the status reports were due on Friday 10/8, you have them all by Monday morning 10/11.

You have status data on tasks 4, 14 and 18, all of which started on the first day of the project. So you'll click on task 4 in the upper half of the window to select it in the upper half of the task entry window you have been using. Click into the lower half of the window and then right-click and select "Work" from the drop down list. As shown in the display below, Sally has completed 45 hours of work on her task and she has 15 hours remaining. You can enter data into any two of the three fields and let the software calculate the third when you click OK.

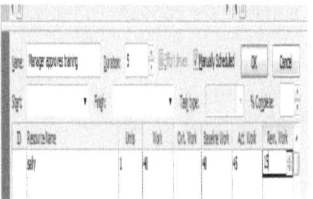

The software has stored the baseline data that the Human Resources Director approved. It had Sally assigned full time with 40 hours of work.

Healthcare Project Essentials

You see that Sally has already worked 45 hours and estimates 15 more for a total of 60. That is 20 hours more than the baseline so you have a variance on this task.

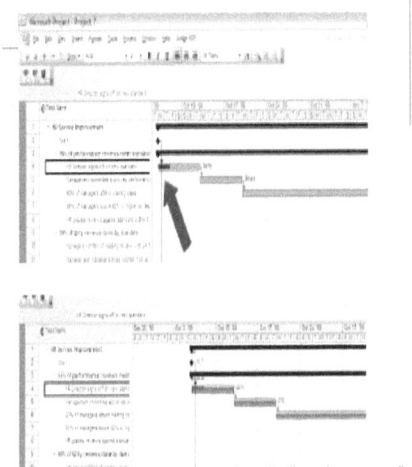

Entering Actual Results

In the upper screen shot, you see Sally's status report on the regular Gantt chart. Inside the Gantt bar, you see a darker progress bar that shows you how far along she is. A better way to look at actuals is with the tracking Gantt, shown in the lower screen shot. If you click on {Gantt chart} and select the {Tracking Gantt} from the drop down menu, you'll see that the Gantt chart has changed. Each task now has two bars. The upper bar is the current schedule and the lower bar is the baseline schedule that you saved earlier.

Healthcare Project Essentials

Technique #11 Problem Solving and Reporting

After you have entered all the data, look at the overall project to see what has happened.

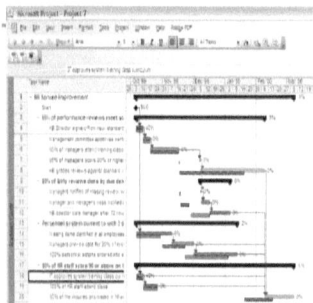

There is slippage in your project plan whenever the top bar (actual) is not aligned with the grey bar (baseline). Note the variance on task #8. That task started later than you planned in the baseline and will finish later too, if you don't take action. Also, note how the slippage on task#8 and the slippage on task #14 have caused their successor tasks to have variances as well. The variance has rippled all the way through the project down to the scope, which is now showing that you will finish two weeks late.

Before starting your analysis, you need to update the schedule. Click on {Project} and {Update Schedule} and then select the option to "reschedule uncompleted work to start after." Then enter the date of the team's status reports as shown below.

You should give the Human Resources Director and the entire project team a printed copy of the tracking Gantt each week. That way they know the challenges the project faces. However, it is important to recall that these are the variances that will occur in the future if you take no action.

While some people may think it sounds good to "crack down hard on every variance," good project managers know that duration estimates can be wrong and that people do encounter unexpected problems. You need to focus your problem solving on real problems that affect the project completion date. As an example, it would be foolish to demand that everyone work overtime to catch up on the slippage. That would waste time and money and have little impact on the project.

Where is the best place to solve the problem? The tendency is to think that you need to take action on the slipping tasks by committing more resources. But adding people to in-progress tasks doesn't always work. The new people have to be "brought up to speed" and that takes time away from doing the job. You may also find that two people can't efficiently do some tasks. Last, it is hard to find additional people who can start work immediately.

Healthcare Project Essentials

On the other hand, you might be able to recapture the earlier slippage by adding people to task 15, task 16 or to both. PMs tend to forget the "downstream" solution, thinking that it is vital to fix the problem in the task where it occurred. Yet it is often easier to acquire the service of additional people starting two or three weeks from now than it is to get them tomorrow.

If you adopt these latter two solutions, you need to propose that corrective action to the Human Resources Director and get her help in securing the additional people. You'll also need her concurrence with the fact that you will be running behind the plan for several weeks until you reach the "catch up" task.

You'll go through this tracking, problem identification/solving and reporting process each week for the duration of the project.

Technique #12 Closing the Project, Making the Next Project Easier

When the project is complete, the project results have been accepted and verified and you've completed your documentation, it is still valuable to close out the project with a "lessons learned" analysis. The point of this analysis is not to revisit every duration overrun in the project. Rather, you want to discuss how well the process of project management worked. During the lessons learned analysis, you'll spend most of your time on the project planning process and try to link problems you've had during the project to issues in your planning process.

Project Closing & Archiving

- Project acceptance: Result verification
- Lessons learned
- Ideas for future projects
- Focus on front-end processes:
  - Scope
  - Requirements
  - Charter & Authorities
- Archive data on how long tasks took to make estimating easier next time

It's easy to blame every overrun on bad people. But the fact of the matter is that you help yourself improve by making sure that your process of managing the project did not contribute to the overrun. You'll examine the clarity of the assignments you gave to people, making sure they really could understand what they were supposed to deliver. You'll examine how well your project charter and its authorities worked. Did managers pull their people off the project despite the agreements you had about time commitments? Were the work estimates you used in the project schedule reasonable or did you fail to consider the complexity of some of the assignments? Were you able to control the changes the hospital administrator made to the project? Did the mechanisms you put in place to limit "scope creep" work effectively?

The answers to these questions are the heart of your lessons learned. You may review these lessons with the Human Resources Director in the hope of making future projects for other hospital administrators more successful. You may also retain the information so that the

Healthcare Project Essentials

next time you develop a project scope and schedule, you can use these examples of problems to make them better.

Another important issue in closing a project is to save the data on each of the tasks; the original estimates and the actual results in terms of how long and how much work it actually took to get the tasks done. This data is invaluable when you are doing estimating for your next project. It doesn't take many months before you have an estimating database that allows you to look for similar tasks and use the actual data as a starting point for your estimating process.

Healthcare Project Essentials

About the Author

Dick Billows, PMP, GCA is President of The Hampton Group, Inc., (4PM.com) specializing in project and program management. He has more than twenty years of project management experience managing hundreds of successful projects as both a management and systems consulting partner with an international accounting firm and internally within a Fortune 100 organization.

His professional career began with two years as a financial analyst on Wall Street followed by six years as a consulting engineer, analyst then project manager, leading implementation projects throughout the US and abroad. Dick served as the Director of Management Systems for a major insurance company, leading a corporate reengineering effort. Then he served as Regional General Manager for the 14 state Rocky Mountain region of a Fortune 100 drug company, managing a portfolio of marketing, system and operational improvement projects that led to a tripling of revenues and profits in two years. He launched numerous new products and several subsidiary business ventures. Next, Dick was the partner-in-charge of Rocky Mountain management consulting for a big ten accounting firm, managing hundreds of installation and system development projects for clients. Dick's project management experience ranges from PC systems for small start-up organizations to network solutions for multi-national companies. More recent deliverables have come with e-commerce and web-based learning systems development.

In 1986, Dick formed the Hampton Group, Inc. and has assisted numerous organizations in their project management including: Siemens, NASA, Intel, Citicorp, Disney, GXS, ConocoPhillips, Health South, Kaiser Permanente, EDS, Hewlett-Packard, Kodak, Marathon Oil, Federal Reserve Bank, Broadcom, Oracle, Bethlehem Steel, Bell South, First Data Corporation and US Dept. of Energy as well as smaller organizations like Candy's Tortilla Factory and Colorado Mountain Development.

Dick was a member of the advisory board that developed the Gartner IT Project Management Certification. Dick has a BA in Economics and Statistics from Johns Hopkins University, an MBA from the University of Colorado and did three years of doctoral work in Organizational Behavior, also at the University of Colorado.

Dick is also the author of: Essentials of Project Management, 11th edition 2013; Project Manager's Knowledge Base, 11th edition 2013; Advanced IT Project Techniques, 6th edition, 2013; Advanced Construction Project Techniques, 5th edition, 2013, Program and Portfolio Management, 9th edition, 2011 and Advanced Healthcare Project Techniques, 3rd edition, 2013.

He is a frequent speaker at Project Management Institute Symposiums and writes the monthly PMTalk newsletter and the 4PM blog.

IT/IS Project Essentials 60

Slide 1

Slides for Visual Learning Review

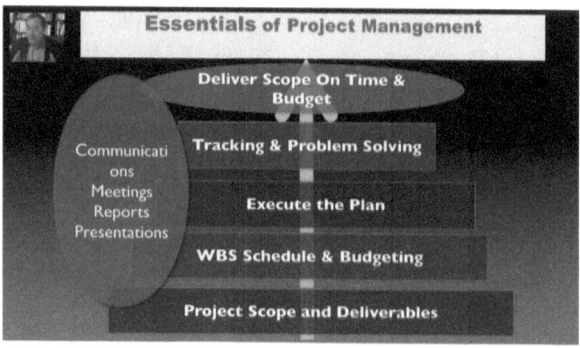

©Copyright 2018 Dick Billows. All Rights Reserved. May not be reproduced in any form without written permission

IT/IS Project Essentials 61

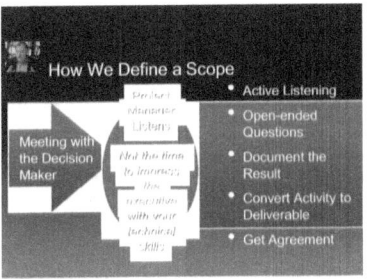

IT/IS Project Essentials 62

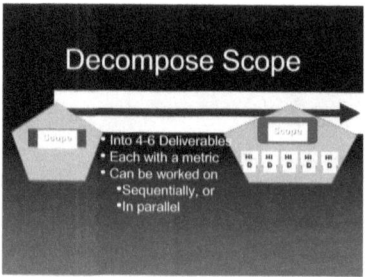

IT/IS Project Essentials 63

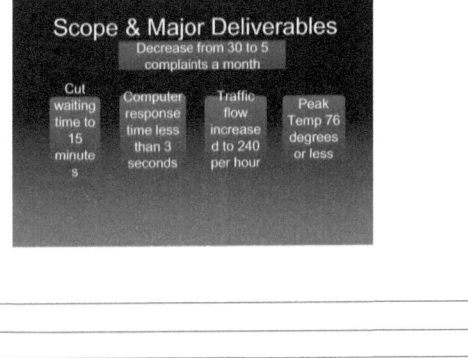

IT/IS Project Essentials 64

Slide 32

IT/IS Project Essentials 65

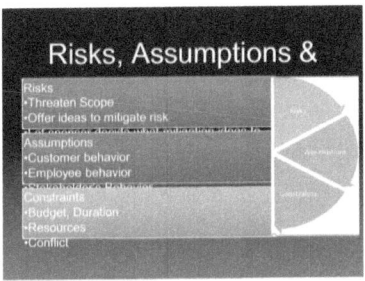

IT/IS Project Essentials 66

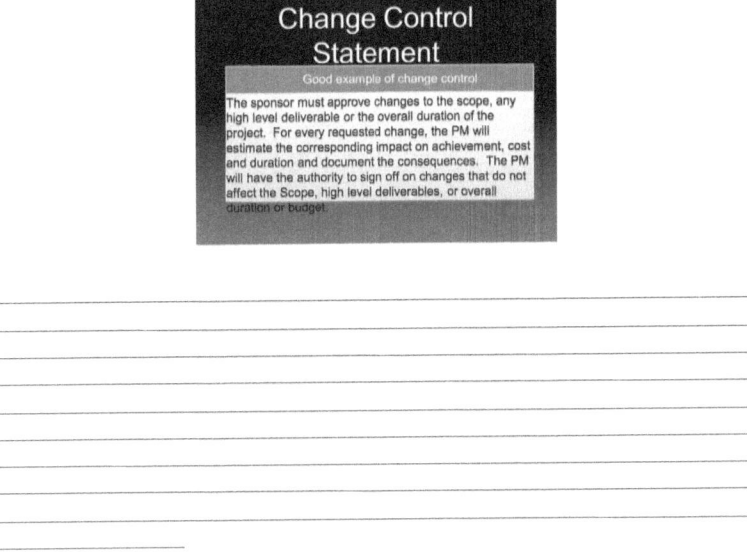

Persuading Extraverts

- Be prepared for them to talk and interact
- Will not sit passively and listen
- Plan for an interactive presentation
- You respond to questions
- Best if they reach the "right" answer themselves

Persuading Introverts

- Details in advance so they have time to process the info
- Don't push for a decision, wait for it; they need time
- They will listen attentively to the details
- Be prepared for detail-oriented questions
- Be sure your detail is flawless

Mixed Audiences

- When your audience includes both introverts and extraverts
    - Design your presentations to meet the needs of each of them
    - Introverts get the detail before the meeting
    - Extraverts are given time to talk during the meeting
    - Extraverts want the big picture
    - Project manager is ready to steer the conversation back on track

IT/IS Project Essentials 71

Slide 9

Body Language

- Extension of our personality
- Show confidence
- Mannerisms to avoid

video

©Copyright 2018 Dick Billows. All Rights Reserved. May not be reproduced in any form without written permission

Communications Plan for Stakeholder

Stakeholder Analysis and Communications Plan		
Stakeholder Name	Personality Type E or I	Individual Communication Plan

IT/IS Project Essentials

Benefits of Visual Aids

Improve listener understanding
- Announce each main point
- Accentuate & illuminate important ideas

Helps audience follow your "train of thought"
- Provide an outline
- Ensure message is immediately evident

Makes your presentation more memorable
- Helps people see what you mean
- Increases the chances that what you said will be

Key is to make the media a second input not a repeat of what you are saying

Work Breakdown
Techniques for creating a strong WBS

| The WBS is not a "to do" list | Crafting "right sized" assignments | Using MS Project to build the WBS |

Wrong Way to Do a WBS

- **Improve Customer Service**
  - Reserve training room
  - Develop training
  - Order snacks for training
  - Everyone attends training
  - Train employees

These are "to do's". We want measured achievements

Right Way to Do a WBS

- 95% customer satisfaction by survey
  - R. Smith approves training materials
  - 100% employees attend training
  - 90% employees score 80% or higher on end of training exam

These are clear success metrics that define expectations

Right Way to Do a WBS

- 95% customer satisfaction by survey
- R. Smith approves training materials
- 100% employees attend training
- 90% employees score 80% or higher on end of training exam

These are clear success metrics that define expectations

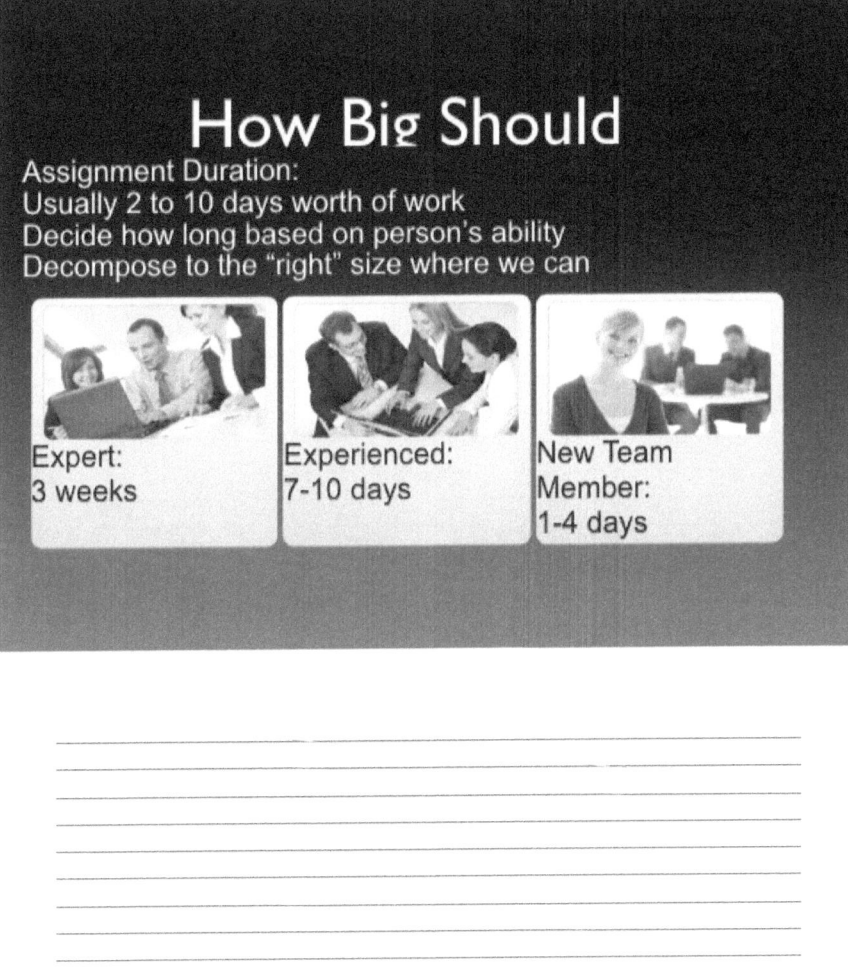

Micro-management Does Not = Tight Control

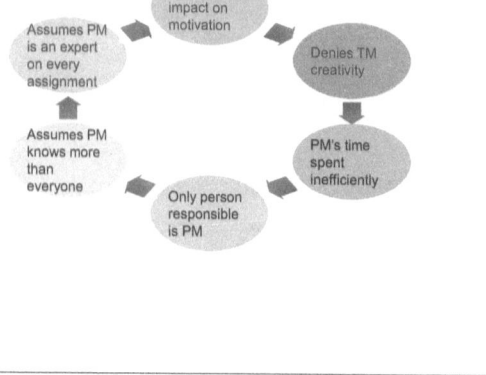

What You've Learned

- How to decompose the WBS
- How to define measured achievements
- Crafting right size assignments
- Using Project software to build the WBS

Rules of Dynamic Scheduling

Dynamic, not static scheduling
- No fixed start or finish dates for tasks
- We let the software calculate them

Tasks
A task's start date is controlled by the finish date of its predecessor(s)

Network
- No danglers
- 1 endpoint
- Every task except summaries have a predecessor

IT/IS Project Essentials 83

Deliverable Network

85% of employees retrieve supplies in less than 2 minutes

Sponsor approves design, plan & budget	System passes acceptance criteria and user accepts it	Reorder quantity set less than 5 out of stocks per month	100% Supply orders pass test on restocking	Fifth HLD
1-1: Managers approve storage design & ordering procedure	2-1: Contractors Sign Agreements	3-1: Department managers approve inventory levels	4-1: Test approved by human resources	5-1:
1-2: Building department approves construction drawings	2-2: Project manager accepts detail design	3-2: Customer approves change in supply inventory cost	4-2: 90% of supply ordering employees attend training	5-2:
1-3: Customer approves plans	2-3: Coding passes unit testing	3-3:	4-3: 100% of supply ordering employees score 85% or higher on test	5-3:
1-4:	2-4: System passes user tests and meets acceptance criteria	3-4:	4-4:	5-4:

IT/IS Project Essentials 84

Slide 7

Risk issues:	Pessimistic Factors	Optimistic Factors
	Employees will not attend training so additional classes	Managers pressure people to attend first class
Assumptions:	Test will measure understanding of the new process	
Documentation & developmental checkpoints	Approval by human resources	

Work (hours/days):	Pessimistic	Best Guess	Optimistic
	50 Hrs	45	35
Estimated Duration:			44.1

Risk & Estimating

IT/IS Project Essentials 86

Essentials of Project Management

- Use critical path to shorten duration and spot tasks that have slack (float)
- Use the software to model options for doing the project faster and cheaper
- Present a plan & tradeoffs for faster & cheaper

IT/IS Project Essentials 87

Critical Path Technique

Analyze the critical path:
- Critical path=longest path. Controls project duration
- Use it to shorten duration:
  - If we shorten duration of a critical path task we shorten project duration

Slide 11

IT/IS Project Essentials 88

Wrong Way to Do a WBS

- **Improve Customer Service**
  - Reserve training room
  - Develop training
  - Order snacks for training
  - Everyone attends training
  - Train employees

These are "to do's"
We want measured achievements

IT/IS Project Essentials 90

IT/IS Project Essentials 91

Modeling Tradeoffs

Options for reducing the duration or the budget
- We shorten the duration by:
  - Adding resources to critical path tasks
  - Reducing the achievement
- We reduce the budget by:
  - Using less expensive resources
  - Reducing the achievement
- We reduce time & cost by reducing scope & deliverables

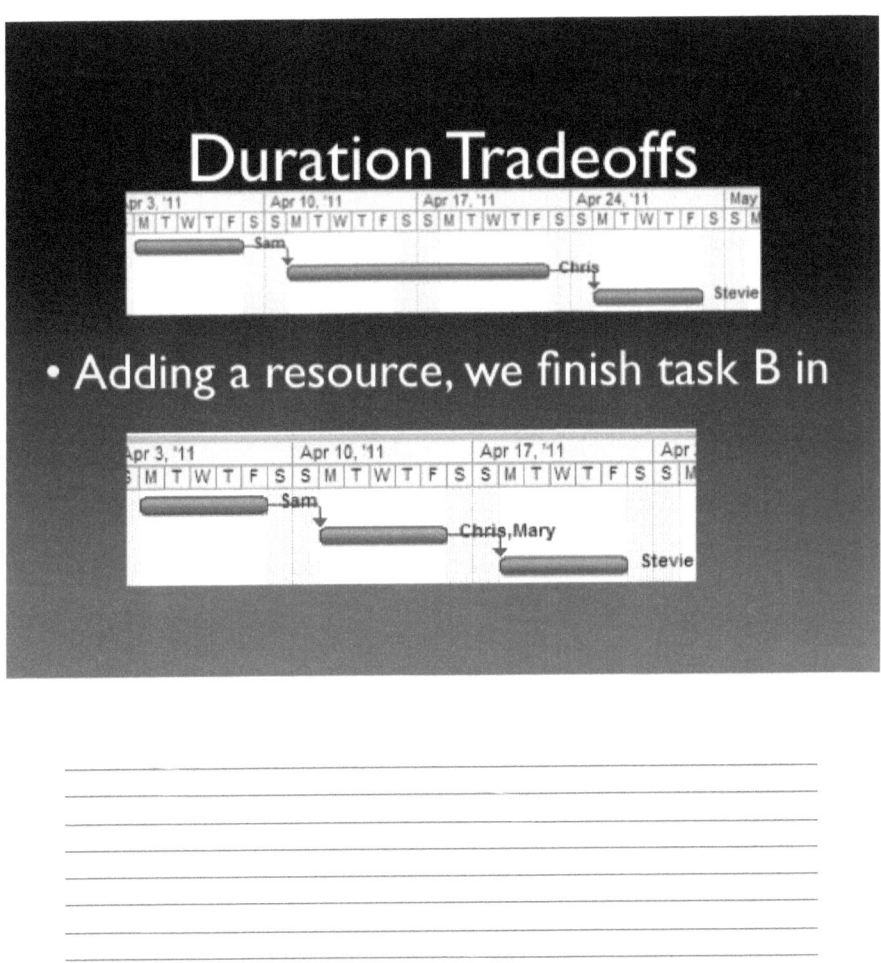

Duration Tradeoffs

- Adding a resource, we finish task B in

Tradeoffs that scale back

Task Name	Total Cost	
<5% of customers call back about the same issue	$4,000.00	

Reduce scope & deliverables to decrease budget & duration

Task Name	Total Cost	
<10% of customers call back about the same issue	$2,000.00	Mary

Slide 19

IT/IS Project Essentials 96

©Copyright 2018 Dick Billows. All Rights Reserved. May not be reproduced in any form without written permission

IT/IS Project Essentials 97

Slide 20

IT/IS Project Essentials 98

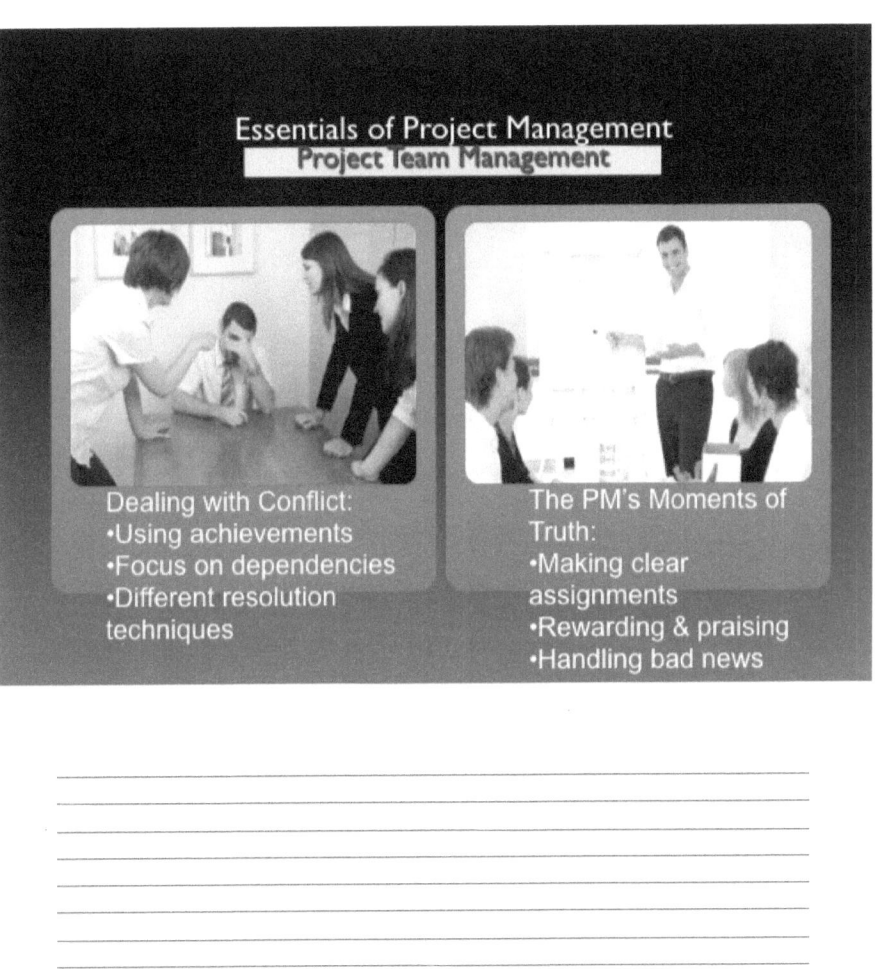

IT/IS Project Essentials 100

2nd Moment of Truth: Feedback

The PM's praise has value when:
- Public
- Consistent & justified
- Measurable & defined beforehand
- Specific about outstanding

The PM's praise loses value if:
- Given to everyone
- No tie to demonstrated performance
- Given to avoid hurt feelings

IT/IS Project Essentials 101

Slide 25

©Copyright 2018 Dick Billows. All Rights Reserved. May not be reproduced in any form without written permission

IT/IS Project Essentials 102

Slide 26

PM Style & Conflict

- Anticipate Conflict
- ID Sources of Conflict in the Charter
- When Conflict Flares: Separate Personality from Issues
- Preserve the Achievement Contract

©Copyright 2018 Dick Billows. All Rights Reserved. May not be reproduced in any form without written permission

Techniques

Different Techniques for Dealing with Different Situations

- Compromising - Everybody wins a little in negotiated solution
- Confronting - Take the time to analyze the issue
- Forcing - PM decides and makes it stick
- Smoothing - Avoid the problem, gloss over it
- Withdrawal - PM spends no time on the issue, lets people solve it

IT/IS Project Essentials 104

Compromising

Use when:
- Both parties need to win
- Can take time to craft mutually agreeable solution
- Issue is important enough to justify PM's time

IT/IS Project Essentials 106

Forcing a Solution

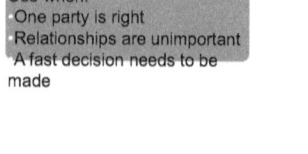

Use when:
- One party is right
- Relationships are unimportant
- A fast decision needs to be made

Withdrawal

Use when:
- One party can't win
- Low stakes
- High stakes but PM unprepared

IT/IS Project Essentials 108

Slide 33

Withdrawal

Use when:
- One party can't win
- Low stakes
- High stakes but PM unprepared

©Copyright 2018 Dick Billows. All Rights Reserved. May not be reproduced in any form without written permission

Focus on Deliverable not Personalities

- They don't have to be friends to finish the deliverable
- Aim to diminish the impact on the project and its deliverables
- Be certain they are seeing beyond personalities to the project and performance issues
- Enforce professional conduct

IT/IS Project Essentials 110

IT/IS Project Essentials 111

Essentials of Project Management Reporting

- Tracking Team Member Progress
- The Estimate to Complete Data Needed for Accurate Status Reports
- Use the Software to Track Progress Before the Status Meeting, not During
- Model Variance & Solutions for the Sponsor

Baseline & Forecasted

Baseline (Originally Approved Schedule/Budget) to Actual
- Basis of comparison

We gather status data from the team members who report hours worked by task and an estimate of hours to complete the task. We enter that data into software and assess variances vs. baseline and assess the impact of the actuals on budget and duration of the project

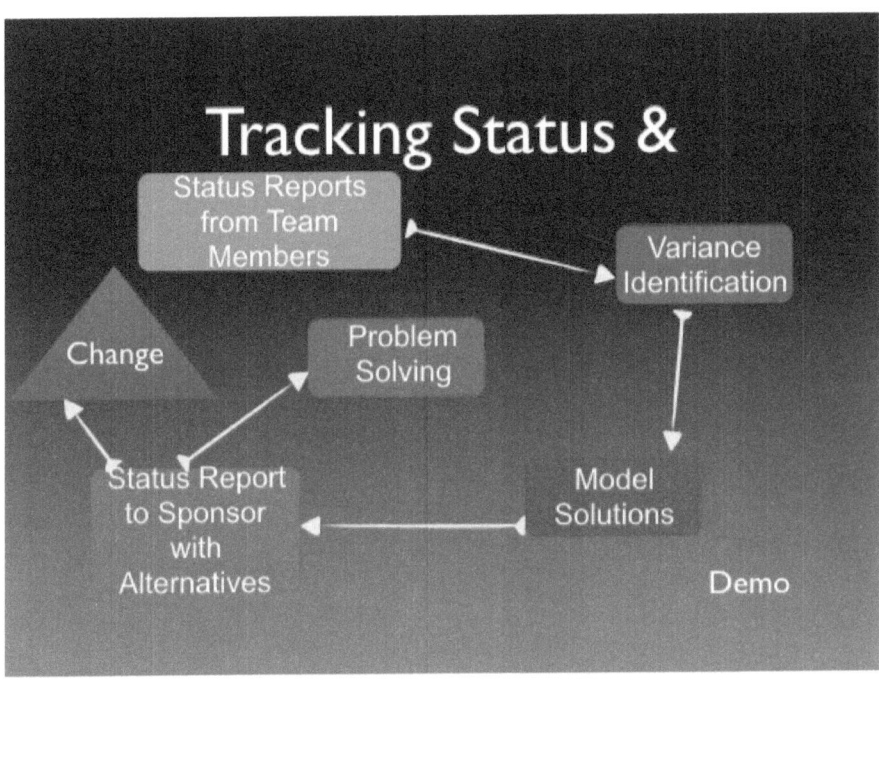

Change Request

- Follow the change control policy in the charter
- PM analyzes impact of change in the software on
  - Scope
  - Duration
  - Cost
  - Risk

Slide 41

IT/IS Project Essentials 115

IT/IS Project Essentials 116

Slide 42

©Copyright 2018 Dick Billows. All Rights Reserved. May not be reproduced in any form without written permission

IT/IS Project Essentials 117

Slide 43

IT/IS Project Essentials 118

Slide 44

Change Request from the Template

Change Request

Project name: supply Room
Submitted by:
Date: 6/23
Approval level: Project sponsor

Brief description of change being requested: Add a work area in the supply room with desk, ethernet connection and printer

Impact on Scope   No impact, not necessary to achieve the scope

Impact on Cost $2000 increase

Impact on Schedule   Adds 3 days to the completion date

Impact on Quality   No impact,

Project manager's evaluation and recommendation on _6_/_24_/____   Reject
Sponsor decision on __/__/__

IT/IS Project Essentials 120

Slide 46

IT/IS Project Essentials 121

Slide 47

IT/IS Project Essentials 122

Slide 48

Slide 49

IT/IS Project Essentials 123

©Copyright 2018 Dick Billows. All Rights Reserved. May not be reproduced in any form without written permission

Status Report from

Status Report Worksheet		Without Corrective Action			Applying Corrective Action
Task Number	Name	Current variance	Forecasted variance	Impact on project cost & duration	Corrective Action Options & Impact
4	1-1: User Managers approve storage	6 days	8 days	4,000	Project sponsor need to force a decision by the managers on the new design

About the Author

Dick Billows, PMP, GCA is President of The Hampton Group, Inc., (4PM.com) specializing in project and program management. He has more than twenty years of project management experience managing hundreds of successful projects as both a management and systems consulting partner with an international accounting firm and internally within a Fortune 100 organization.

His professional career began with two years as a financial analyst on Wall Street followed by six years as a consulting engineer, analyst then project manager, leading implementation projects throughout the US and abroad. Dick served as the Director of Management Systems for a major insurance company, leading a corporate reengineering effort. Then he served as Regional General Manager for the 14 state Rocky Mountain region of a Fortune 100 drug company, managing a portfolio of marketing, system and operational improvement projects that led to a tripling of revenues and profits in two years. He launched numerous new products and several subsidiary business ventures. Next, Dick was the partner-in-charge of Rocky Mountain management consulting for a big ten accounting firm, managing hundreds of installation and system development projects for clients. Dick's project management experience ranges from PC systems for small start-up organizations to network solutions for multi-national companies. More recent deliverables have come with e-commerce and web-based learning systems development.

In 1986, Dick formed the Hampton Group, Inc. and has assisted numerous organizations in their project management including: Siemens, NASA, Intel, Citicorp, Disney, GXS, ConocoPhillips, Health South, Kaiser Permanente, EDS, Hewlett-Packard, Kodak, Marathon Oil, Federal Reserve Bank, Broadcom ,Oracle, Bethlehem Steel, Bell South, First Data Corporation and US Dept. of Energy as well as smaller organizations like Candy's Tortilla Factory and Colorado Mountain Development.

Dick was a member of the advisory board that developed the Gartner IT Project Management Certification. Dick has a BA in Economics and Statistics from Johns Hopkins University, an MBA from the University of Colorado and did three years of doctoral work in Organizational Behavior, also at the University of Colorado.

Dick is also the author of: Essentials of Project Management, 11th edition 2013; Project Manager's Knowledge Base, 11th edition 2013; Advanced IT Project Techniques, 6th edition, 2013; Advanced Construction Project Techniques, 5th edition, 2013, Program and Portfolio Management, 9th edition, 2011 and Advanced Healthcare Project Techniques, 3rd edition, 2013.

He is a frequent speaker at Project Management Institute Symposiums and writes the monthly PMTalk newsletter and the 4PM blog. About the Author

IT/IS Project Essentials 126

Dick Billows, PMP, GCA is President of The Hampton Group, Inc., (4PM.com) specializing in project and program management. He has more than twenty years of project management experience managing hundreds of successful projects as both a management and systems consulting partner with an international accounting firm and internally within a Fortune 100 organization.

His professional career began with two years as a financial analyst on Wall Street followed by six years as a consulting engineer, analyst then project manager, leading implementation projects throughout the US and abroad. Dick served as the Director of Management Systems for a major insurance company, leading a corporate reengineering effort. Then he served as Regional General Manager for the 14 state Rocky Mountain region of a Fortune 100 drug company, managing a portfolio of marketing, system and operational improvement projects that led to a tripling of revenues and profits in two years. He launched numerous new products and several subsidiary business ventures. Next, Dick was the partner-in-charge of Rocky Mountain management consulting for a big ten accounting firm, managing hundreds of installation and system development projects for clients. Dick's project management experience ranges from PC systems for small start-up organizations to network solutions for multi-national companies. More recent deliverables have come with e-commerce and web-based learning systems development.

In 1986, Dick formed the Hampton Group, Inc. and has assisted numerous organizations in their project management including: Siemens, Intel, NASA, Citicorp, Disney, ConocoPhillips, Health South, Kaiser Permanente, EDS, Hewlett-Packard, Kodak, GXS, Marathon Oil, Federal Reserve Bank, Broadcom, Oracle, Bethlehem Steel, Bell South, First Data Corporation and US Dept. of Energy as well as smaller organizations like Candy's Tortilla Factory and Colorado Mountain Development.

Dick was a member of the advisory board that developed the Gartner IT Project Management Certification. Dick has a BA in Economics and Statistics from Johns Hopkins University, an MBA from the University of Colorado and did three years of doctoral work in Organizational Behavior, also at the University of Colorado.

Dick is also the author of: Essentials of Project Management, 11th edition 2013; Project Manager's Knowledge Base, 11th edition 2013; Advanced IT Project Techniques, 6th edition, 2013; Advanced Construction Project Techniques, 5th edition, 2013, Program and Portfolio Management, 9th edition, 2011 and Advanced Healthcare Project Techniques, 3rd edition, 2013.

He is a frequent speaker at Project Management Institute Symposiums and writes the monthly PMTalk newsletter and the 4PM blog.

©Copyright 2018 Dick Billows. All Rights Reserved. May not be reproduced in any form without written permission

www.ingramcontent.com/pod-product-compliance
Lightning Source LLC
Chambersburg PA
CBHW031432210526
45464CB00005B/2162